WHAT IS LA HISPANIDAD?

JOE R. AND TERESA LOZANO LONG SERIES IN
LATIN AMERICAN AND LATINO ART AND CULTURE

WHAT IS LA HISPANIDAD?

A conversation

ILAN STAVANS AND IVÁN JAKSIĆ

UNIVERSITY OF TEXAS PRESS

Austin

Translation of "To Roosevelt" by Rubén Darío is used
courtesy of Steven F. White and Greg Simon.
Translations of "Poetry" and "Ode to Tropical Agriculture"
by Frances López-Morillas from *Selected Writings of Andrés
Bello* are used by permission of Oxford University Press, Inc.

Requests for permission to reproduce material from this
work should be sent to:
Permissions
University of Texas Press
P.O. Box 7819
Austin, TX 78713-7819
www.utexas.edu/utpress/about/bpermission.html

♾The paper used in this book meets the minimum
requirements of ANSI/NISO Z39.48-1992 (R1997)
(Permanence of Paper).

LIBRARY OF CONGRESS CATALOGING-IN-PUBLICATION DATA
Stavans, Ilan.
    What is la hispanidad? : a conversation / Ilan Stavans and
Iván Jaksić. — 1st ed.
        p.   cm. — (Joe R. and Teresa Lozano Long series in
Latin American and Latino art and culture)
        Includes index.
        ISBN 978-0-292-71938-5 (cloth : alk. paper)
        ISBN 978-0-292-72561-4 (pbk. : alk. paper)
        1. Civilization, Hispanic.   2. Pan-Hispanism.
I. Jaksić, Iván, 1954–   II. Title.
CB226.W43   2011
946—dc22
                                                    2010024165

A mi querido maestro Gonzalo Sobejano
—I.S.

A Jorge J. E. Gracia,
quien me hizo pensar en esto, y más
—I.J.

Far from being one story, human history in its aggregate resembles a great cauldron whose perpetually simmering surface sees incessant collisions of innumerable particles, each moving in their own orbits, along trajectories that intersect at an infinite number of points.

RYSZARD KAPUŚCIŃSKI,
TRAVELS WITH HERODOTUS (2007)

CONTENTS

WHAT IS LA HISPANIDAD?

IVÁN JAKSIĆ: The purpose of this series of six conversations plus an epilogue is to investigate the parameters of Hispanic civilization. I presume our dialogue will be descriptive rather than prescriptive. In other words, my idea is that the two of us engage in a discussion with the hopes of mapping out this rather elusive field, as it has evolved historically.

ILAN STAVANS: A tall order. But I like to pursue large aspirations. In his 1864 poem on Abraham Ibn Ezra, Robert Browning wrote: "What I aspired to be, / And was not, comforts me."

IJ: I should be more specific about the inception of this book. It begins in 2007, when, unbeknownst to me, the New York office of the publishing house Palgrave Macmillan sent you the manuscript of my book *The Hispanic World and American Intellectual Life, 1820–1880.* Thus began a dialogue that, done mostly electronically and by phone, with several tête-à-têtes in Santiago, Chile—all in all over a period of eighteen months—resulted in extensive exchanges about the interconnections of North and South in the Americas, as well as East and West between the two shores that frame the Atlantic Ocean. Casey Kittrell, an editor at the University of Texas Press, wholeheartedly embraced the prospect of turning the conversations into a unified book. Neal Sokol created the index.

IS: Given the scope of the endeavor, I propose dividing our conversations, to the extent possible, into thematic chapters.

IJ: Let's start by setting the parameters of our topic, then concentrating on various areas pertaining to the shaping of the concept of Hispanic civilization. For instance, the emergence of Spain during the Renaissance as a unified kingdom and then as an empire, the foundation of the Hispanic American republics in the nineteenth century, and the strategies the latter undertook to define their national identity in response to those of Spain, France, and the United States.

IS: Another topic to discuss should be language as a tool in the formation of Hispanic identity.

IJ: Our inquiry should survey the intellectual debates of the independence period in Latin America between 1810 and 1865, and the way the nations of the Western Hemisphere developed in social, political, and religious ways during the twentieth century.

IS: But I want to have a chapter about pop culture: *telenovelas, fútbol,* music, the carnival . . . I want us to move away from an elitist realm that concentrates exclusively on ideas and meditate on the impact of figures like Tin-Tan and Corín Tellado. In addition, it is an imperative to focus our attention on Latinos in the United States. This minority, the nation's largest and fastest-growing, is an integral part of Hispanic civilization. In 2005 one out of every ten *hispanos* lived north of the Rio Grande.

IJ: Our task should be ambitious.

IS: Yes, but I'm sure it will also be entertaining. Also, it's better to try and fail than not to try and then wonder what our limits were. I find the task we've set for ourselves timely, for at the outset of the twenty-first century, Hispanic civilization seems to be in a state of constant mutation. Of course, it has always been in transition. But the almost half a billion people always seem to be asking: Who am I? Where do I come from? What makes me different? Indeed, at the heart of our identity, in my eyes, is uncertainty about our condition. Why are our political systems fragile? Other civilizations are more pragmatic and forward-looking. These types of questions have been asked by thinkers like José Enrique Rodó in *Ariel* (1900), Ezequiel Martínez Estrada in *X-Ray of the Pampa* (1933), and Octavio Paz in *The Labyrinth of Solitude* (1950).

IJ: Finally, each of us should feel free to combine the personal with the analytic. I'm hoping to produce a narrative that flows easily, one that is at once enlightening, intellectually entertaining, and grounded on personal experiences.

IS: I agree.

IJ: Let me start by pointing out the ubiquity of the word hispanidad. Why this prevalence? What does the word mean? When did the term emerge? In what context? With what scope?

IS: I'm also struck by the way it has become a banner.

IJ: For what?

IS: I'm not sure. An elusive sense of unity.

IJ: Among whom?

IS: For instance, I come across it when I watch the U.S.-based Spanish-language networks Univision and Telemundo. It is also present in the festivities of Columbus Day, *el día de la hispanidad.*

IJ: I mentioned Hispanic civilization. Perhaps you and I need define what a civilization is, don't you think? People use the word casually. Yet in the work of political scientists like the late Samuel Huntington, author of *The Clash of Civilizations* (1996), it acquires an ominous sound.

IS: The sociological, psychological, religious, political, cultural, and linguistic dimensions of a people conform a civilization, but the concept is more than the sum of its parts. A civilization is a way of looking at life, a way of smelling, hearing, tasting, and touching. And, more important even, a way of thinking, for each civilization thinks of the world in a different fashion.

IJ: Let's move on to the matronymic, then: hispanidad.

IS: Should it be spelled with a capital *H*?

IJ: In English, yes.

IS: But capitalizing the *H* stressed all the more its pamphleteering nature. For Hispanic civilization, as I understand it, is one thing, and la hispanidad something altogether different. Thus, I suggest, for our own purposes, spelling it in lowercase.

IJ: How is Hispanic civilization different from la hispanidad?

IS: Hispanidad is an ideological stance, maybe even an argumentative approach, that is, the use of the specific elements of Hispanic civilization for a political purpose. In Spanish, *una profesión de fe.* It's fascinating to me to follow the etymology of the term *hispanidad.* It's absent in Sebastián de Covarrubias Orozco's *Tesoro de la lengua castellana o española* (1611), the first "official" lexicon in Spain; this absence is thought-provoking, among other reasons, because Covarrubias's volume, published under the imprimatur of the Holy Office of the Inquisition, appeared in between the first and second parts of Miguel de Cervantes's *Don Quixote of La Mancha.* Over time, Don Quixote and Sancho Panza have become emblems of la hispanidad. But the concept didn't play a role in their author's welt-anschauung. There was no such a thing in the period.

Hispanismo and other related words make an appearance in the *Diccionario de autoridades* (1734), which would become the basis of the lexicon of the Real Academia Española. *Hispanismo* is defined, in part, thusly (in its eighteenth-century spelling): "Modo de hablar particular y privativo de la Lengua Española; como Entendido por hombre que Entiende" (A particular and unique way of speaking the Spanish language; understood as by an educated man). And *Hispano* is said to be "lo mismo que Español. Es voz poética" (a synonym of *español*. It's a poetic voice). The *Diccionario,* then, establishes a parallel between Spanish (i.e., Iberian) and *Hispano* and equates the term with a way of speaking (but not with a way of being).

More recently, the *Diccionario de la lengua española,* in its twenty-second edition, contains the following definitions:

> Hispánico, -ca: 1. Perteneciente o relativo a España. 2. Perteneciente o relativo a la antigua Hispania o a los pueblos que formaron parte de ella y a los que nacieron de estos pueblos en épocas posteriores. 3. Perteneciente o relativo a la lengua y la cultura españolas.

> [Hispánico, -ca: 1. Belonging or pertaining to Spain. 2. Belonging or pertaining to ancient Hispania or to the people that formed part of it and to those people that were born out of it in successive epochs. 3. Belonging or pertaining to the Spanish language and culture.]

> Hispanidad: 1. Carácter genérico de todos los pueblos de lengua y cultura hispánica. 2. Conjunto y comunidad de los pueblos hispánicos. 3. Hispanismo.

> [Hispanidad: 1. Generic character of the people belonging to Hispanic language and culture. 2. Gathering and community of the Hispanic people. 3. Hispanism.]

> Hispanismo: 1. Giro o modo de hablar propio y privativo de la lengua española. 2. Vocablo o giro de esta lengua empleado en otra.

3. Empleo de vocablos y giros españoles en distinto idioma. 4. Afición al estudio de las lenguas, literaturas o cultura hispánicas.

[Hispanism: 1. Usage or mode of speech belonging or pertaining to the Spanish language. 2. Word or turn of this language used in another. 3. Use of Spanish words or expressions in a different language. 4. Interest in the study of Hispanic languages, literatures and culture.]

There's also the archaic proper adjective *hispanense,* but the dictionary states that it is no longer in use and that when it was used in the past, it applied strictly to people. In other words, *hispanense* was taken to be an adjective referring to Spanish folks.

IJ: And yet, the term *hispanidad,* as mentioned before, is laden with numerous connotations.

IS: Numerous and conflicting, it seems to me. In the chronological effort by lexicographers just mentioned, the word emerged in the early eighteenth century as relative to speech. But by the nineteenth century, the period in which the Real Academia Española consolidated its institutional standing, it reached wider into the epistemological realm, denoting a condition: *lo hispánico,* things exclusive to Hispanic civilization.

IJ: As I recall, there was even a highly political concept of la hispanidad in the twentieth century, put forth by the regime of Francisco Franco in Spain, for propaganda purposes, whereby *lo hispánico* meant "Catholic and anticommunist." What was your first encounter with the concept?

IS: In Mexico, where I was born and raised, I don't remember ever pondering the concept. Granted, I left the country at twenty-five to become a newspaper correspondent in New York. It was only once I was living abroad, in La Gran Manzana, the Big Apple—that enormous fruit market of *hispanidades*—that I began thinking about it in any serious fashion.

IJ: In your memoir *On Borrowed Words,* you explore the way culture, in particular language, shaped your education.

IS: Indeed, in Mexico I was raised Jewish, that is, a member of a small cultural minority. That identity defined us in every sense of the word. We attended private school, in my case a Yiddish-language one, where the calendar honored Mexican as well as Jewish holidays. On Independence Day, September 16, for instance, there were no classes. Cinco de Mayo, commemorating the Battle of Puebla against the French, was also a day off. But so were Rosh Hashanah and Yom Kippur. Our last names sounded different. And although my family was an exception, Jews lived in relatively wealthy neighborhoods like La Condesa, Hipódromo, Polanco, Las Lomas, and Tecamachalco. In addition, we spoke Yiddish and Hebrew. That is, as a minority we had our own space, time, and words. It wasn't until I moved to New York, in the mid-eighties, that I became Mexican, and, by extension, Hispanic.

IJ: Was this surprising or unexpected?

IS: I felt my hispanidad defining me in an elastic way, as if I had suddenly been splashed with a bucket of cold water. I had come to New York to be a newspaper correspondent and also go to graduate school. That I spoke Yiddish was inconsequential. More than inconsequential, it was useless. Aside from English, which was my ticket to mainstream society, using my Spanish allowed me to become a member of another minority. I used it with Puerto Ricans, Cubans, Dominicans, Colombians, Venezuelans, Nicaraguans, Salvadorans, Costa Ricans, and other Mexicans. Each of us used a different, idiosyncratic Spanish. But the linguistic differences that characterized our speech were less important than the similarities: we were all *hispanos.*

IJ: *Hispanos* and not *hispánicos.*

IS: Yes, *hispano:* a lazy collective noun, a variation of the English *Hispanic.*

IJ: Yet the term *Latino*—and, hence, *la latinidad*—has acquired more currency. When did *Hispanic* start to be used? And how about *Latino?*

IS: The term *Hispanic* came along in the United States, in an official manner, in the early seventies, during the Nixon administration. It was the first time the Feds openly referred to Latinos and, at first at least, the usage was perceived as a triumph. It was, after all, a statement of recognition. After centuries of being ignored as a de facto minority, the Nixon administration finally named the unnamable: the Hispanic community. Richard Rodriguez refers to this moment in his book *Brown: The Last Discovery of America* (2002).

IJ: There is the issue of names, official or not, and the issue of national origin or experience, both of which add to the complexity of being *hispano.*

IS: When in 1993 I edited, along with Harold Augenbraum, the anthology *Growing Up Latino,* one of the first of its kind, for the U.S. publisher Houghton Mifflin, the working title was *Growing Up Hispanic.* Upon requesting permissions, we received severe warnings from a couple of potential contributors (Sandra Cisneros, among them) who refused to participate until and unless the word *Hispanic* was replaced by something else. But by what? One option Sandra Cisneros and others endorsed was *Latino;* actually, she wanted *Latina and Latino.* I thoroughly disliked that option; it wasn't a title but a political manifesto. Gloria Anzaldúa wanted the book to be called *Growing Up Mestizo and Mestiza.*

IJ: Really!

IS: It was painful. The in-house editor, Marc Jaffe, laughed about the whole name game. To satisfy everyone, should the volume be called *Growing Up Hispanic, Latino and Latina, Mestizo and Mestiza, and* _____ (fill in the blank)? The consensus was that we needed to embrace the most neutral, politically correct word: *Latino.*

IJ: Were you pleased with the outcome?

IS: Not in the least.

IJ: Why?

IS: I don't like the term *Latino.* To me it's as evasive as the term *Latin America.* This reminds me of a joke that circulated years ago, when the first George Bush was in office and his vice president was Dan Quayle, a Republican former senator from the state of Indiana not known for his high IQ. Quayle was about to tour Latin America. At one point he gave a news conference in which he was asked what preparation was he making for the trip. He answered that in order to better understand Latin American political leaders, he was brushing up on his Latin.

IJ: It's a favorite misconception, just like the one implying that tourists to Mexico need to buy a dictionary of "Mexican" in order to understand the basics.

IS: Seriously, though, what's Latin in Latin America—Roman law?

IJ: You must know where it came from and at what point it started to be current . . .

IS: During the second half of the nineteenth century, a group of Spanish American exiles in Paris articulated the concept, *la América Latina,* as an emblem of unity. This was, clearly, a tribute to Bolívar's *Gran Colombia* and a way to play against the emerging hemispheric presence of the United States as the powerful neighbor up north. Bolívar used the name *Colombia* in honor of Christopher Columbus, preferring that reference to that of Amerigo Vespucci. The region was known as *las Indias Occidentales.* And, during the colonial period, it had names that emphasized the freshness of the continent, *la Nueva España* among them. Yet *América Latina*—or its variant, *Latinoamérica*—has Eurocentric connotations. Its detractors perceive it as anti-indigenous and even racist. Borges, who was politically conservative, never used the term. In his view, it was a cover-up for the false homogeneity that supposedly permeates the Western Hemisphere. As it happens, neither did his friend, the Mexican essayist, poet, diplomat, and Hellenist Alfonso Reyes, use it. For that matter, nor did Borges's other non-Argentine colleague, the Dominican intellectual Pedro Henríquez Ureña, who suggested that we talk about *la América Hispana* and *la América Portuguesa,* embracing language as the ultimate identifier. (Borges edited an anthology of Argentine poetry with Henríquez Ureña. And with compatriots like Adolfo Bioy Casares and Silvina Ocampo he edited volumes on Argentine stories, as well as anthologies of fantastic literature from around the globe. Intriguingly, he never published an anthology of Latin American literature.)

IJ: So, there was resistance to the *Latin* in the Americas. When did it become more accepted or even widely used?

IS: It was, clearly, a matter of generations. By the early twentieth century, *América Latina* still generated discomfort. However, the Colombian essayist Germán Arciniegas embraced it. So did the Venezuelan novelist Arturo Uslar Pietri. By midcentury, figures like Octavio Paz, Gabriel García Márquez, Julio Cortázar, and Mario Vargas Llosa didn't find it problematic.

IJ: In his book *The Buried Mirror* (1992), Carlos Fuentes suggested an alternative: *Indo-Afro-Ibero América.*

IS: In my estimation, that's worse. It's not really a name but a slogan. Who in the world can say such tongue twister in a single breath? How about *Indo-Afro-Ibero-Luso-Mestizo-Judeo-Arábigo-Católico-Nipón-Germánico-* _____ (fill in the blank) *América?*

IJ: Intellectuals in the region might react to these categories, but people in general don't seem to be too worried about them. They are who they are ...

IS: *Ehye asher ehye.*

IJ: Yet these matters are intensely debated in U.S. academic circles.

IS: We intellectuals have the false belief that our discussions reflect the will of the masses. It is true, as the eighteenth-century German thinker Johann Gottfried von Herder once suggested, that a single sentence conjured by a writer in an isolated room can change the whole world. Yet when judged by the level of self-importance of intellectuals, one would conclude that the world is constantly being transformed by passing, insignificant thoughts.

IJ: However, there is little doubt that the perception of Latin America is different when one discusses it from afar.

IS: I fully agree. The fact that you and I are analyzing it in English, while you're in Santiago, on the western side of South America, and I'm in Amherst and Wellfleet, in New England, surely colors our conclusions. More so, we two are children of immigrants, yours from the former Yugoslavia, mine from Poland and the Ukraine. And for a variety of reasons, both of us left our respective countries of birth—Chile and Mexico—immigrating to the United States ...

IJ: ... where we became Hispanic.

IS: Or Latino. What was your experience as a Latino in the United States?

IJ: My experience moving to the United States was similar to yours. I had a strong sense of national, in this case Chilean, identity, but soon after I arrived I realized that my sense of self was challenged by a larger and stronger community to which I also belonged, *la comunidad hispana*. In some ways, it was like going back to an ethereal sense of belonging to something larger than a narrow national community. I was born at the very end of the world, in the city of Punta Arenas by the Strait of Magellan, where many immigrants lived, and where several languages were spoken, though always in intimate circles, not publicly. I would hear Serbo-Croatian at home, English and

German uttered here and there, but my father always insisted that we, his children, were Chilean, and that meant Spanish-speaking. I can't even begin to describe how strong that sense was, as the school system and the strong military presence in that part of the country instilled it in us. And how incongruous! For when I moved to Santiago, the capital, at age eleven, I was a foreigner among my peers: my accent and vocabulary were different, in fact closer to the Argentine variant than to the dominant Spanish of the central valley of Chile, where most Chileans live. That was my first shock, the first time I realized that I was Chilean, yet not quite. I tried very hard to assimilate, making all the necessary adjustments in language and demeanor. But something was missing: an environment where I could really be at home. Except for short visits, I never returned to my hometown to live.

IS: Did you feel spiritually disjointed?

IJ: Just as you describe in *On Borrowed Words* when going back to Mexico for visits, I could tell there was a real rupture there. At the same time, this early experience helped me when at the age of nineteen, and in rapid succession, I lived through the military coup of 1973, escaped to Argentina in 1974, and returned to Chile only briefly, to leave again, this time for a period of thirty years in the United States. I have written elsewhere about all this, but let me emphasize here just how puzzling and enriching it was for me to become a part of *la comunidad hispana* (it was not *latina,* at least not at the time) in the United States. My closest friends were Puerto Rican, and through them I met a wide spectrum of *hispanos,* from hardworking *boricuas* (from the Indian name of the island—Borinquen) in the Bronx, to artists and writers in Greenwich Village, to longterm exiles from different Latin American countries. I was fascinated by their facility to switch languages, and I did my best to try to understand the process. Pedro Pietri's "Puerto Rican Obituary" became my favorite poem, as a true window into the islander experience in New York and beyond. In Buffalo, where I lived for some time, *hispanos* from different countries, or born in the States, gave me a sense of home and community.

IS: Did you have role models?

IJ: My mentor in graduate school was the Cuban Jorge Gracia, a very distinguished scholar, so that it was not just the food, the language, and the music that are so often cited to describe hispanidad, but true intellectual engagement, that became a fundamental part of this new sense of belonging. His work was primarily on metaphysics, but he was also a pioneer in the study of Latin American philosophy. So we worked together for many years analyzing the thought of various thinkers, until we came up with our coedited *Filosofía e identidad cultural en América Latina,* which we put together between the late seventies and early eighties, though it did not come out until 1988. I cannot describe the thrill of meeting with him, week after week, studying texts and putting them in both historical and philosophical context. I felt I was entering a new world. That was when I decided that my field would be the history of ideas, which it still is. I do not mean to romanticize all of this, for there was a much darker side to being *hispano* in the United States, and I was also struggling with my strong sense of being a Chilean national, despite being persecuted by the Pinochet regime and treated as persona non grata in my own country. But that's another story. Once in the States, I found that I was exposed to all sorts of experiences, including a very significant Hispanic component. But I had to find my own way. There were no clear points of encounter for all of us Latinos.

IS: I find it intriguing that in the United States, October 12 is a holiday known as Columbus Day. What is celebrated? Apparently, the naming of the Americas, that is, the anniversary of Christopher Columbus's arrival in the Americas, which, historically, took place, according to the Julian calendar, on October 12, 1492, and on October 21, 1492, in the modern Gregorian calendar. In other words, since the Gregorian calendar is the most widely used in the world today—based on the traditional Incarnation year of Jesus Christ, hence known as anno Domini, it was first proposed by the Calabrian doctor Aloysius Lilius and decreed by Pope Gregory XIII, after whom it was named, on February 24, 1582, by papal bull *Inter gravissimas*—we should commemorate the arrival of the Genoese admiral about ten days later than we do. However, the central question isn't the mistake that surrounds the date itself but the confusion about what is being celebrated. In Mexico and some parts of Latin America, the name is dramatically different: Día de la Raza. In Costa Rica it is called Día de las Culturas; in Colombia and the Bahamas, Discovery Day; in Hawaii, Discoverer's Day; and the newly renamed (as of

2002) Día de la Resistencia Indígena (Day of Indigenous Resistance) in Venezuela.

IJ: How about in Spain? What do people celebrate on October 12?

IS: Día Nacional, National Day. The emphasis is obvious. As Spain reached beyond its boundaries, its cultural modes made its population believe their horizons were wider. That is what imperialism is about: the belief that your country's self ought to be expansive, global, encompassing other people's daily routine. Starting shortly after Christopher Columbus's return to the Iberian Peninsula from his first voyage across the Atlantic, as the support of Queen Isabella solidified, Spain ratified its imperial quest. That quest has antecedents: for example, the struggle for the diplomatic unification of the kingdoms of Aragon and Castile. In the Americas, the term *Día de la Raza* didn't acquire currency until the nineteenth century, as the wars of independence spread across the continent. Yet the idea of a homogenized continental civilization, *la civilización hispánica,* might reach even further.

IJ: All the way back to El Cid, I believe.

IS: El Campeador. Tell me about your encounter with the legend.

IJ: I must have been eight or nine years old when I heard a radio program in which a panel queried a contestant on the intricacies of *The Poem of the Cid,* also known in English as *The Song of the Cid,* the oldest extant Spanish epic poem written by the Abbot Peter, presumably in the early thirteenth century. It had been a laborious process, with many competing, but there was just one contestant left. Naturally, most listeners wanted him to win, but the questions were very specific and required a command of the poem that was just staggering. To make a long story short, the man won, to our collective joy, but there were several matters that intrigued me. First of all was the story, full of powerful characters and a vigorous assonant rhyme. Second was the level of knowledge: that there would be people, without advanced degrees, or even widespread recognition, who would know so much about a medieval Spanish poem consisting of 3,730 verses, no less. Something stuck in my mind that made me think of la hispanidad: how we could relate, from such distances of time and space, to a foundational story such as El Cid? Impressive. There must be some fundamental values embedded in the poem so as to endure in the far distant corners of the Hispanic world to this day.

IS: I've always found it reductive, for lack of a better word, to teach courses on Latin America in U.S. academic institutions. Does Latin America truly have enough elements in common to justify a sense of unity? Is this unity an invention of a bunch of intellectuals and diplomats?

IJ: There is quite a bit of that. I mean, like toasts at embassy parties or syrupy speeches by visiting VIPs. There is always something that can be said about unity, however empty or misleading it might be. But when you have to teach, and teach the region as a whole over a semester or even a quarter of the academic year, things change quite radically. You have to go beyond the rhetoric and make a serious attempt to provide coherence to the different ways in which regions split from the Spanish Empire and built their own national political and cultural identities. It is quite a challenge to meet this need, of providing a sense of what happened in terms of fragmentation and difference, while at the same time showing patterns in the historical development of nations. For this purpose, I taught for many years, and continue to teach, a course called "The Emergence of Nations in Latin America," wherein I discuss how countries went through this process and managed to build remarkably similar institutions. I find, then, that it is possible to talk about unity, but with many caveats.

IS: Something similar might be said about publishing endeavors. Publishers in the United States and Europe see the Hispanic world, and Latin America in particular, as a block for which they allocate a limited number of annual titles. The covers are designed with stereotypical flair: the jungle, parrots and other exotic birds, butterflies, military figures, et cetera. The style these publishers endorse is magical realism. They want readers to perceive Latin America as a civilization where reality and dreams are intertwined.

IJ: These views are so hard to change! What you are saying reminds me of a respected senior colleague of mine, Fredrick B. Pike, who wrote a book titled *The United States and Latin America: Myths and Stereotypes of Civilization and Nature* (1992). It was a very important iconoclastic book published by the University of Texas Press, but people continue to generalize along the lines you mentioned, as if Pike and others had not made persuasive arguments to show a more complex picture. Stereotypes are hard to get rid of, especially when they go back so far and so deep into the American imagination.

IS: I can't tell you how often I've come across friends from south of the border who say that any deviation from that stylistic norm results in rejection. The case of Latino writers in the United States suggests another form of confinement.

IJ: You have recently published *The Norton Anthology of Latino Literature* (2010).

IS: A long, arduous process that took over a decade. I'm hoping the overall impact of the anthology will be eye-opening because whenever I talk to New York editors about this literature, they seem to have frighteningly narrow views. Manuscripts need to be about the ghetto, alienation, drugs, prison, and, ultimately, survival through personal redemption.

IJ: Yet there is something to say about the way mainstream academic publishers like Oxford University Press have become more sophisticated. Take your *Oxford Book of Latin American Essays* and its counterpart, Roberto González Echevarría's *Oxford Book of Latin American Short Stories* (both 1997). Or else think of the Oxford Library of Latin America, for which I edited an anthology of Andrés Bello's writings. These houses used to focus primarily on politics, revolutions, and all sort of catastrophes.

IS: Takes on social deprivation and political upheaval.

IJ: Yes, exactly. But now they go deeper. The Oxford Library of Latin America has published over thirty works or anthologies by lesser-known (I mean in the U.S.) classics, nineteenth-century figures like Fray Servando Teresa de Mier, Joaquim Machado de Assis, and Clorinda Matto de Turner.

IS: So, do you feel Hispanic, Iván?

IJ: Yes, I do. My father was the son of immigrants from Croatia, but on my mother's side the family had been in Chile for centuries. I slowly discovered that a part of me had much to do with the immigrant experience, but that has never detracted in any way from my consistent identification, at a deep personal level, as a member of the Hispanic world. People of my generation in Chile learned how to navigate other countries, languages, and cultures. We were a small, insular country, and chances are that I would not have left Chile had it not been for the military coup in 1973. But even after three decades of continuous residence abroad, something has always remained with me, a sense that I belong to a particular group of people, regardless of nation, who speak the language and share views about life and world. It is not an exclusionary sense, but it only emerges with people who share the same experience, the same history, and who continue to build personal and social interactions on that basis. Before I left Chile, I felt strongly Chilean and only vaguely Hispanic. But in the United States I discovered how wonderful and enriching it was to be a part of a much larger community.

IS: What does the elusive sense of la hispanidad personally mean to you?

IJ: That we share a common language, and that despite independence from Spain and the resulting fragmentation of our countries, we continue to understand each other and bring the language to new levels of artistry. I have always been inspired by the work of Andrés Bello, who set out to preserve Castilian Spanish after independence but insisted on the peculiarities and legitimacy of local variants. Let me quote one of his passages from *Grammar of the Spanish Language* (1847): "I do not claim to write for Spaniards. My lessons are aimed at my brothers, the inhabitants of Spanish America. I believe that the preservation of our forefathers' tongue in all possible purity is important, as a providential means of communication and a fraternal link among the various nations of Spanish origin scattered over the two continents. But what I presume to recommend to them is not a superstitious purism." He succeeded spectacularly, in the sense that the Real Academia Española acknowledged his points and his contributions, and that his grammar is still the most used in Spanish America.

IS: As I mentioned before, when I go to the soccer stadium or when I turn on the TV to a Spanish-language network, I'm struck by the manipulation of la hispanidad done subtly during sports events, on music shows, and in commercials. The corporate media, it seems to me, is eager for the audience to be infused with a feeling of unity.

IJ: How so?

IS: Unity sells products. If you have a homogenized audience, you're able to influence its shared needs. A fractured body politic is less malleable. During the World Cup, for instance, TV commentators stress the existence of a Hispanic fan base that amounts to more than 400 million people worldwide and that, thanks to the athletes, the differences among, say, the Argentine, the Uruguayan, the

Colombian, the Ecuadorian, the Paraguayan, and the Mexican teams might be minimized in favor of *el fervor latino*.

IJ: I suggest holding our discussion of *el fervor latino* for a later portion of the conversation. First let's place that shared need, as you call it, in historical context by looking at the emergence of Spain as a modern nation.

IS: An awkwardly modern nation.

IVÁN JAKSIĆ: You used the adjective *awkward* to describe Spain as a modern nation. I want to focus on it as the root of things Hispanic.

ILAN STAVANS: Then let's start with the term *casticismo,* about which I'm in awe.

IJ: Why?

IS: *Casticismo* is a posture, a caricature. It is an attitude that probably started in the eighteenth century in Spain as a response to *la cultura afrancesada,* the French influence in music, literature, and the arts. It was also a reaction to the Enlightenment: a denial of open, free-flowing ideas. *Casticismo* is a synonym of *reactionary.* It manifested itself everywhere in social behavior: food, fashion, and parlance. To be *castizo* meant to be an authentic Spaniard of impeccable breeding, which the Real Academia defines as *de buen origen y casta.* Remember, it was among the most obscurantist periods in that nation's history, a categorical refutation of liberal European culture.

IJ: An authentic Spaniard! Isn't that an exaggeration? I mean, considering the history of the country?

IS: It is worth recalling at this point a superb moment in Borges's "Pierre Menard, Author of the *Quixote*" (1939). The story, you might recall, is about an early twentieth-century French symbolist whose major task in life, the endeavor he wants to be remembered by, is to rewrite *Don Quixote.* Menard is no plagiarist—he doesn't want to copy Cervantes's masterpiece. He wants to write it again as if it were the first time. That is, he won't use a copy of Cervantes's novel for his purposes. His theory is that if a novel of that caliber is able to show up, through inspiration, once to an author, why can't it appear twice in the exact same format? Although Menard only rewrites a small number of chapters, it's enough to prove his point. Borges, a genius, compares Cervantes's text to Menard's and—surprise!—they are identical. Yet in the narrator's opinion, Menard's version is richer, subtler than Cervantes's because he needed to look at seventeenth-century Iberian culture from outside: to learn its language, to re-create its environment.

The moment I want to recall comes when the narrator tells the reader that, in the hands of a mediocre author, the rewriting would have been filled with stereotypes designed to give the flavor of the epoch: autos-da-fé, gypsies, and so on, the sort of artifact placed for tourists to get the message with which Flaubert overstuffed *Salammbô,* his historical novel about the Roman Empire. Fortunately, Menard is more measured, because, in my opinion, he is an outsider looking in and decidedly not a *castizo.*

IJ: Correct me if I'm wrong, but *casticismo* doesn't seem to have a counterpart in Latin America.

IS: No, I believe you're right; it doesn't have a counterpart. I've known *castizos* in Mexico, but they are second-rate replicas.

IJ: And a replica is already a copy.

IS: There's a class referent, of course. Etymologically, the word *castizo* might come from *casta.* Thus, it was connected with a backward-looking, urban middle class. By the late nineteenth and early twentieth centuries, it emitted a terrible odor.

IJ: How so?

IS: José Ortega y Gasset, praising novelist Leopoldo Alas (a.k.a. Clarín), author of *La regenta* (1885), said that "escritor casticista significa en mi léxico una forma del deshonor literario, quiero decir, una de las muchas maneras, de las infinitas maneras entre que un poeta puede elegir para no serlo." An approximate English translation: "to be a writer in the *castizo* mode is to fall into literary dishonor, a way for a poet not to be a true poet."

IJ: So we're talking about two different things.

IS: Indeed, hispanidad and *casticismo* couldn't be more different.

IJ: To fully understand these concepts, and our entire subject, it is useful to look into history. It would be shortsighted to treat la hispanidad as if it emerged after Latin American independence, just as it is to view the Latino experience as if it began the moment we moved to the United States. I believe we need to go much further back, and for that we can really benefit from a historical perspective.

Many historians emphasize catastrophic breaks, ruptures, turning points, as the true stuff of history, but the field would be incomplete without a look into continuities. Many Latin Americans at the time of independence wanted to believe that a genuine Latin American experience began only then, and wished to obliterate the past.

IS: How about Spain?

IJ: Even liberal Spaniards, after the death of Ferdinand VII in 1833, wanted to forget the imperial experience from the Habsburgs to the Bourbons as a bad nightmare from which they needed to awaken. But the reality is that the past that some wanted gone had in turn other historical roots. This is why it is important to see the development of historical events, and especially culture, from a long-term perspective. We're lucky in the Hispanic world that we had such an intellectual giant as Andrés Bello exploring the roots of hispanidad, even though he was surrounded by very vociferous individuals who wanted to do away with the hated Spanish past. He went far back into the origins of the Spanish language, which he considered *the* moment when la hispanidad began. I am referring to his research, pioneering at the time, on *The Poem of the Cid*. One might argue with him about whether hispanidad is so closely tied to the emergence of the Spanish language, at least as recorded in this wonderful thirteenth-century epic poem. But at least he called attention to the origins of what and who we are today.

IS: La Reconquista in Spain might be the cathartic historical moment.

IJ: Absolutely, but with ups and downs and fits and starts of bellicose energy and peaceful interaction with Arabs. Eight centuries is a long time, and it could not have been all war. But there was a certain mystique about gaining territory, inch by inch, against a powerful enemy that had enormous cultural assets. For a time, Spanish Christians were little more than bands of marauding guerrillas as described in *La chanson de Roland*. But religion and European military assistance eventually turned the tide in favor of the Spanish Christians. There are some very powerful symbols of the time, such as *The Poem of the Cid*. All the elements of a vibrant sense of nationality are there. But contrary to what many Spanish nationalists may claim or what the nineteenth-century American Hispanist George Ticknor would assert, the Spanish sense of nationality was not exceptional or entirely indigenous. It incorporated many elements of the language, the laws, and the literature of a pan-European spectrum of sources. One only has to look at *Las siete partidas,* the seven-part code of law compiled under the aegis of Alfonso X, to realize how strongly it was based on Roman law. And without these legal foundations it is impossible to understand how Spain was able to catapult itself from a collection of weak and divided kingdoms into a powerful worldwide empire. So religion, law, and a growing sense of nationality, forged over centuries of peace and struggle, are really the foundations of the extraordinary historical experience underpinning hispanidad.

IS: The Catholic monarchs Ferdinand and Isabella, are they central to this process?

IJ: These monarchs understood with singular clarity the advantages of unity in a political, religious, and geographical sense. They led the final push to eliminate the last remnants of the Arab presence in the peninsula, the kingdom of Granada, even though it was already a tributary to the Spanish monarchy. The monarchs mobilized resources of a magnitude never seen before, and secured the loyalty and support of wide segments of the population, as well as the church and the European community. Isabella was the senior partner, as queen of Castile, the most powerful region in Spain. Ferdinand was the head of a much smaller kingdom, Aragon, but he brought enormous political talent into the partnership. All evidence points to a fruitful collaboration in which love was not absent. They were truly an admirable couple who nevertheless left a less-than-admirable legacy.

IS: You're referring to the institutionalization of Catholicism, I suppose.

IJ: Catholicism was a powerful force in La Reconquista, as well as in the lives and spirituality of the Spanish population. But Ferdinand and Isabella used the church for political aims, reforming the regular orders, introducing the Inquisition, and securing the Patronato Real, the royal patronage that gave them almost complete control over the church. They did it as a fundamental component of their idea of statecraft. They viewed and used Catholicism as a powerful symbol of unity that gave Spain a sense of mission and nationality. Yet the Catholic Church would soon exercise a power they had not envisioned, especially after both monarchs died.

IS: This is best exemplified by the expulsion of the Jews on March 31, 1492, and the Arabs ten years later. La Reconquista was an extraordinary project of unification, that is, homogenization: one nation, one religion, one language. The text itself (a.k.a. the Alhambra Decree) proclaiming the expulsion reads in part:

> [We are informed of] the great damage to the Christians which has resulted and results from the participation, conversation, communication which they have held and do hold with the Jews, of whom it is proved that they always attempt by whatever ways and means they can to subvert and detract faithful Christians from our holy Catholic faith and separate them from it and attract and pervert them to their cursed belief and opinion, instructing them in the ceremonies and observances of their law, convening assemblies where they read to them and teach them what they must believe and observe according to their law, taking care to circumcise them and their sons, giving them books from which they can recite their prayers and declaring the fasts which they have to fast and joining with them to read and teach them the stories of their law, notifying them of the Passover before its date, informing them about what they must observe and do, giving them and removing from their houses the unleavened bread and the meat that has been slaughtered according to their rite, teaching them about what they must avoid in foods and other things to observe in their religion, and in persuading them as best they can to keep and observe the Law of Moses, and in giving them to understand that there is no other religion or truth [except] that, and this is proved by the many [statements] and confessions both of the Jews themselves and also of those who were corrupted and deceived by them. And all of this has brought great damage and injury to our holy Catholic faith.

Catholics are portrayed as wronged by Jewish mores. What is feared the most is the objectionable activities of the *conversos,* or converts. By the last decade of the fifteenth century, and all the more so after the expulsion, eventually postponed for July 31, 1492, this new class had reached higher echelons in Spanish society, especially in the realms of finance, culture, and religion. The presence of *conversos* generated much angst. Did they truly believe in Christ? Were they still loyal to the Jewish faith? The angst forced Iberian society to exist in a permanent state of duality. The expulsion was an attempt to heal this wound in the Spanish heart.

IJ: Let me add that aside from the arbitrariness and cruelty of the measure, it was a misguided policy that did more harm than good to the country. It deprived Spain of a learned and loyal segment of the population and introduced an edge of intolerance and zealotry that would take centuries to change, making hispanidad synonymous with intolerant Catholicism when it could have been, from the start, an inclusive concept. The talent that left the country at the time ultimately enriched the life of other nations at the expense of Spain.

IS: The year 1492 also marks the capitulation of Granada and the surrender of the Moors.

IJ: As in the case of the Jews, the persecution of the Moors was part of the political design of the monarchy and later the empire. They felt compelled to create an enemy within so that Spain could keep defining itself as solidly Catholic. One can provide many historical explanations for these measures, but ultimately it was a cruel and counterproductive way of building a sense of nation. It made no sense economically and it was ethically reprehensible, like many similar situations before and after.

IS: I believe you're referring to the concept of "the enemy within," which became current not too long ago in so-called *marrano* studies. In his book *The Other Within* (2009), Yirmiyahu Yovel, who teaches philosophy at the New School and has published distinguished studies on Spinoza, devotes his attention to what he describes as "the split identity" of the *marranos,* as the Jewish converts to Christianity were derogatorily called, disseminated across the Mediterranean Basin, northern Africa, the Middle East, and the Americas before and after the Spanish expulsion in 1492. In other words, he analyzed the effect that being the easy target you talked about generated in those who were singled out by the establishment as well as their descendants.

IJ: I heard the concept of "the enemy within" from Richard Herr, a distinguished scholar of Spain, when I organized a seminar on hispanidad at the time of the quincentennial, in 1992. He saw it as a constant in Spanish history.

IS: Yes, Yovel took it from Herr and pushed it in different directions. Yovel's central argument is that, in their cosmopolitanism, the *marranos* (whom he also refers to, mistakenly, as *conversos,* crypto-Jews, and New Christians, as if there were no subtle differences between these rubrics) were the ferment that allowed for modernity to emerge in Western civilization. According to Yovel, they were a new class of citizen who, among other things, were skeptical, committed themselves to rationalism, embraced individual initiative and achievement, and endorsed a private restlessness in cultural and religious terms. Furthermore, in their new sensibility, they were, alone and as a group, the discoverers of subjectivity and the inner mind. The *marranos* were also the builders of the concept of self and, in their work (intellectual, scientific, and trade), placed an emphasis on irony, bifurcation, and linguistic allusions.

In other words, the double consciousness that is the staple of modern times is a *marrano* creation. Among those considered "the enemy within" were poets like João Pinto Delgado and Miguel (Daniel Levi) de Barrios; mystics like Luis de Carvajal the Younger; and heretics Gabriel (Uriel) de Costa, Juan (Daniel) de Prado, and Benedetto (Baruch) de Spinoza. Yovel affirms that the *marrano* constellation took shape after the Iberian cohabitation of Christianity, Judaism, and Islam collapsed. It created a nation outside the nation, a borderless camaraderie of those described as having impure blood who, through secrecy, forged worldwide business patterns. What united them, Yovel believes, was not religion but their bastard condition, "their shared origin and common *converso* experience and predicament."

Groucho Marx once claimed that he did not wish to belong to any club that would accept him as a member. In Yovel's view, the *marrano* club was more sophisticated. While never openly acknowledged, it fostered a culture of support to people who at times didn't even know they belonged to the club.

IJ: This issue seems to make you restless, Ilan.

IS: Well, some scholars of medieval Spain attribute to *marranos* portentous qualities that are closer to metaphor than to reality. For instance, some of the characteristics Yovel ascribes to *marranos* are surely not exclusive to their weltanschauung. Leo Strauss, in his collection *Persecution and the Art of Writing* (1952), included an essay on the coded style of *The Guide for the Perplexed.* Maimonides' philosophical treatise dates back to the twelfth century, long before the *marrano* dilemma was shaped. My point is that the strategy of expounding a dangerous viewpoint through a veil obviously isn't limited to the post-Sephardic paradigm. And neither is it surviving in the shadows of an establishment that forbids religious freedom. In any case, the idea of the *marranos* constructing a *nationless nation* is enchanting. (I've italicized the term to show how enamored I am of it.)

Yovel dislikes the term *diaspora* to refer to this construction. A diaspora, he says, "implies there is a center, and one's identity somehow revolved around it," but that "Iberia was neither the actual nor the normative center" of the *marranos.* He is wrong on this account (the word *diaspora* comes from the Greek, "a scattering of seeds," and while it has an origin, it doesn't necessarily have a center). However, Yovel's assertion is not really about the term itself but about its alternative. He suggests *archipelago,* "a system of separate but linked islands." Or better, *constellation,* "a group of large and small stars with varying degrees of brightness, forming a loose system without an organizing core." In either case, what he is after is a vision of the *marrano* universe as engaged yet fractured, polyphonic yet interrupted.

IJ: The point is that medieval Spain united by expelling those who didn't fit its political agenda.

IS: Yes, the Spain of La Reconquista was committed to unity. A century later it called in the troops to fight in two fronts, the external and the domestic. In the former, it placed the blame on the British, which brought down the "Invincible Armada" in 1588, and the Turks, who were seen not only as a political and commercial opponent but also as a religious menace. And in the latter, it vilified Moors and Jews as national enemies. In other words, the mentality remained intact.

IJ: Yes, national enemies . . .

IS: In the preceding chapter you talked about El Cid. This example of the *mester de juglaría,* which philologist Ramón Menéndez Pidal reinvented through his lucid scholarship for the modern reader, celebrates the vigor of Iberian Catholicism in its effort to defeat the Muslim infidels during the time of the Reconquista. El Cid returns from exile in order to reclaim his honor. For honor is what matters to him: *la honradez.* Although the *cantares* have a decidedly realistic tone, the volume isn't a historical document. A number of facts are changed—the names of El Cid's daughters, for instance.

IJ: Yet Cervantes is often considered a better guide to understanding Spanish history.

IS: Cervantes's life is an invaluable road map to understanding the ghosts Spain was fighting in the late sixteenth and early seventeenth centuries. Cervantes was a mediocre playwright. His envy toward Lope de Vega, the wunderkind of Golden Age *comedias,* is patent in various corners of his oeuvre. And Cervantes was an unsuccessful writer of pastoral novels. His self-esteem depended on his career as a soldier. Having fought in the Battle of Lepanto, which, in his own view, was Spain's defining historical moment, and where he lost the use of his left arm, he nurtured a feeling of patriotism that comes across vividly in the discussion between Don Quixote and Sancho, in part 1, chapter 38, on the preeminence of arms over letters, as well as in the novella "The Captive's Tale." Just as Borges did three centuries later, Cervantes considered a soldier's path more worthy than that of a poet. Upon his own return from captivity in Algiers, Cervantes tried his luck with his pen—with miserable results. He became a tax collector, a profession in which he also did poorly, for it is known that he was accused of embezzlement, apparently even spending time in jail. His magnum opus, *Don Quixote of La Mancha,* was therefore an act of survival. Or at least an attempt at reinventing himself. By the way, I'm in love with Salvador Dalí's drawings of Don Quixote and Sancho.

IJ: A decade ago, from 1999 to 2001, you edited a special issue of *Hopscotch: A Cultural Review*—a journal published by Duke University Press—that was devoted to the various translations of *Don Quixote* into English. You also included illustrations of the sorrowful knight done in different historical periods as well as quotes from celebrated intellectuals on Cervantes's masterpiece.

IS: I don't remember if I included anything by Dalí. I should have . . . The Surrealist painter was tickled by the caballero and his squire. Over the years, Dalí made a number of drawings, etchings, and aquatints. The earliest dates back to the sixties. I'm awed by the one that has a red Medusa engraved in the knight's shining armor. The actual face of Don Quixote—Christlike—is small in comparison with his enormous helmet.

IJ: I've seen it. The landscape appears to be absolutely empty . . .

IS: As if the only thing that mattered was the knight himself, which is true.

IJ: In addition to *The Poem of the Cid,* I believe that Cervantes's work provides us with a great literary guide for understanding the uniqueness of the Hispanic experience. Although I grew up reading and hearing about *Don Quixote,* I became intensely interested in this book only after I moved to the United States. As you know, he is a very familiar figure even there.

IS: There have been a total of nineteen full translations into English of Cervantes's masterpiece, by all accounts a considerable number. (By the way, Shakespeare and Cervantes died on the same date in 1616, but they lived by different calendars, Julian and Gregorian. As it happens, Cervantes died ten days before Shakespeare.)

IJ: Remarkable, but is there something more than the traditional stereotype about the humorous, somewhat foolish idealist who is supposed to epitomize Hispanic culture, along with his grotesque but likeable sidekick Sancho Panza? When I reread the novel in the United States, I saw the drama behind the story, and also Cervantes's powerful reflection about a country that had lost the ideals of La Reconquista and was already on its way to becoming an obsolete, second-rate empire full of bureaucrats and opportunists. A couple of things had happened in between: I was deeply interested in the role of technology in history, and to me *Don Quixote* provided wonderful evidence about the irruption of a whole range of artifacts in sixteenth-century Spain. Everyone knows about the windmills, but there are quite a few other technological innovations, which Don Quixote uniformly considers giants, monsters, or "enchanted" creatures.

IS: Indeed, Cervantes's novel is, among other things, a superb register of the impact of modernity on Spanish society.

IJ: In a sarcastic way, Cervantes acknowledged the entrance of modern technology into a traditional society, and wished to illustrate what it did to the mentality of an old hidalgo, motivated by chivalric values, representing old Spain. But the central technological innovation that really structures the book is the printing press, which makes possible the practice of reading. Don Quixote goes crazy reading books, until he finds out where they come from: a very prosaic printing shop. It is then that his undoing begins, and he retreats home to die. Related to printing, and usually in opposition to it, is orality, which is represented by Sancho with his nonstop stream of proverbs and sayings.

IS: Carlos Fuentes once wrote an essay called "Cervantes, o la crítica de la lectura" (1976), in which he states that *Don Quixote* is, more than anything else, a book about the act—that is, the art—of reading.

IJ: Yes, an insightful essay, but it does not address the more prosaic aspects of the technological revolution that affected Spain at the time. I wrote an essay called "Don Quijote's Encounter with Technology" for the journal *Cervantes* in 1994. I was convinced then, and I still am, that Cervantes put his finger on a central element of the Hispanic experience: how a society with such origins and history as Spain faces and deals with technological modernity. This is obviously not confined to Spain, but what I am saying is that Spain already had a firm set of values and a sophisticated language with which to record the significance of the technological manifestations of modernity. My ultimate test, however, was forwards, and across the ocean: How did and do Latin Americans deal with modernity? Do they also see in technology a threat to Hispanic values and culture? Sure enough, I identified a whole range of Latin American intellectuals who joined Don Quixote, but rather less humorously, in condemning technological modernity. I wrote an essay called "The Machine and the Spirit" for the *Revista de Estudios Hispánicos* in 1996, where I tried to call attention to this very strong and persistent thread connecting Hispanic values on both sides of the Atlantic.

IS: *Don Quixote* is truly full of meanings.

IJ: It's your favorite book, isn't it?

IS: I've thought more on *Don Quixote of La Mancha* than about any other book.

IJ: As Irving Leonard documented in his *Books of the Brave* (1949), it was widely read in the New World. Let's explore the impact of Spain in the Americas during the colonial period.

IS: The so-called Black Legend—attributed to Fray Bartolomé de Las Casas, among the first political activists from Europe in the New World—turns out to be the glue connecting the various Americas together.

IJ: Las Casas has become an obligatory point of reference. His admirable and unflagging support for the Indians was clouded only by his support for the introduction of African slavery, a position for which the U.S. Hispanists of the nineteenth century castigated him endlessly. But in Latin America he became a revered figure: he represented a kinder face to the bloody history of the conquest. He became a symbol of alliance between Indians, well-meaning Europeans, and criollos. His being a religious figure added yet another powerful component to the emerging sense of national identity after independence, when religion still occupied a central place in Latin American politics and society. That is, all the ingredients of postcolonial reconciliation are there, epitomized in this one major figure.

Never mind that he was used for political purposes and that the real Las Casas, or the context of his times, has been distorted beyond recognition. There is also a very ambiguous legacy, in that Las Casas introduced some of the most enduring stereotypes about Hispanic culture. As you stated, by exaggerating the cruelties of the Spaniards, he launched the Black Legend, *la leyenda negra,* which became the standard European view on the Hispanic world. He is at the very basis of the characterization of Spanish culture as hopelessly despotic and inquisitorial. Julián Juderías described this development with caustic accuracy in his *La leyenda negra* (1914). Philip Wayne Powell, in an unjustly forgotten work, has also called attention to the persistence of *la leyenda negra* in the United States, in his *Tree of Hate: Propaganda and Prejudices Affecting United States Relations with the Hispanic World* (1971).

IS: What would be the connection between the Black Legend and the concept of hispanidad?

IJ: Whenever there is a persistent condemnation and distortion of your culture and history, the tendency is to combat such views with the tools of research and reason, on the one hand, and an assertion of the positive values which you believe are being ignored, on the other. Clearly, the more exaggerated claims of the Black Legend have led to a search for a deeper understanding of our history and culture. These days, I think, there is enough information, for all those who care, to demolish the fundamental assumptions of *la leyenda negra.*

IS: To switch to another pervasive theme, let us talk for a minute about Miguel de Unamuno, who once wrote an essay called "En torno al casticismo."

IJ: Indeed, you are referring to a series of articles that he prepared mostly in 1895, just before the Spanish-American War deprived Spain of its last remaining overseas possessions. Unamuno was already talking about Spain's "malaise," lamenting how much of the old national, historical spirit had been lost. By *casticismo* he meant the nucleus of a Spanish identity that originated in the middle ages, which in due course provided the nation with a singular force, a drive to achieve great deeds that became synonymous with *lo español.* That is, while he traced the origins of *casticismo* in Old Castile, he celebrated its inclusiveness, believing that it eventually encompassed all of Spain. His illustrations through literature show a most impressive erudition. It is a great piece, marred only by his irrepressible verbosity: the whole essay could have been distilled to a few pages.

IS: "Irrepressible verbosity"—I like your expression. I remember the first time I read one of Ramón del Valle-Inclán's *esperpentos.* The word itself still makes me giggle. María Moliner's *Diccionario de uso del español* compares an *esperpento* with a *disparate.*

IJ: A *disparate,* at least in my part of the world, has two connotations: one is the *garabato,* crass and even dirty language; the other is the sense of gibberish, exaggeration, and nonsense.

IS: Moliner's definition of *disparate* is "cosa absurda, falsa, increíble o sin sentido que se dice por equivocación," an absurd, false, incredible, meaningless thing said by mistake. That is, a Freudian slip. But these kinds of slips vary from *cultura* to *cultura,* don't you think?

IJ: Absolutely. I would disagree with the "*equivocación*" part. A *disparate* need not be either an error or a Freudian slip. If I say to someone in Chile that he or she is saying a *disparate,* I mean that he or she is talking nonsense or deliberately saying something false for polemical purposes.

IS: I'm convinced a *disparate,* in a *castizo* environment, is quite different from a Freudian slip in a Puritan environment.

IJ: I agree. In the latter environment a Freudian slip means saying something that you did not plan on saying that reveals your true feelings, often quite hidden and even inappropriate at a conscious, verbal level.

IS: María Moliner also suggests that *esperpento* was a particular modality of theater created by Valle-Inclán in which reality was deformed so as to find its most absurd and grotesque qualities. The version I saw of *Tirano Banderas* was Brechtian: everything was made to feel cartoonlike. Clearly the director wanted the audience to know that what Valle-Inclán had imagined was not real life per se but his far-fetched interpretation of it.

IJ: Hispanic humor also exaggerates and distorts reality, but I would not equate it exactly with *esperpento* or even the baroque. Hispanic humor, more often than not, is a play on words, a comedy of mistakes that results from confusions in language use or double entendres. I believe that your work on Cantinflas illustrates this quite well. In Chile our humor can be a bit dry, but it is uniformly based on language, its complex meanings and how the use and misuse of some words, depending on context, can create hilarious situations. They are of the sort illustrated in Alice's encounter with the Mouse. When she asks the critter about his situation, he responds, "Mine is a long and a sad tale!" Puzzled, she replies, "It *is* a long tail, certainly, . . . but why do you call it sad?" We are constantly making humor out of such confusions of language. In the days of Pinochet, people liked to tell a joke about the general, who was not known for his subtlety, upon a visit to a famous museum and in front of a famous though abstract portrait, say, by Picasso. An aide whispers something for him to say for the benefit of the cameras: "¡Qué cara, qué gesto!" (What a face, what an expression!), which the general mishears and pronounces as "¿Qué carajo es esto?" (What the f——is this?)

IS: Would you say that Hispanic humor is baroque?

IJ: It would take a comprehensive survey of humor in several countries, but what I know of those that I have visited is that jokes tend to be short and to the point, often involving some grievance of a political or social sort (although far too many concern sex). And the way tends to be the manipulation of words to suit a given situation. This does not exclude the baroque, but it mostly involves the ingenuousness to deceive, or to contrive outcomes, through words. In *The Poem of the Cid,* El Campeador tricks some businessmen into giving him some cash in exchange for a coffer full of sand, which he claims to be gold. The situation is meant to be hilarious, but it is really based on a dark, almost aggressive sense of humor. That the financers are Jewish adds to the perverse humor, as if it is okay to do such a thing because they are Jewish. In the end, El Cid does not pay his debt.

IS: Reflecting on Hispanic humor is like joining an archaeological expedition. It tells much about where we come from.

IJ: Do you believe, with Carl Gustav Jung, that jokes not only reveal our unconscious life but also describe ancestral ways of thinking?

IS: Nah! When it comes to psychoanalysis and its derivations, I'm a skeptic.

IJ: I don't know, Ilan. Jokes really have to do with language. Dreams can perhaps reveal deeply suppressed feelings about the constraints of civilization, as Freud claimed, and jokes might do likewise. But as a means to understand the mind of the first *Homo sapiens,* I also have my doubts.

IS: In other words, studying Spanish jokes is like analyzing the Roman ruins in the Iberian Peninsula. But let me continue with the topic of archaeology. The so-called discovery of Machu Picchu in 1911 by the U.S. historian Hiram Bingham marks a crucial moment for the way the Hispanic world—in this case the Hispanic American world—has been perceived globally. Bingham's claim to have found the lost Inca city, we now know, is mistaken. How could he have "found" something that man already knew about? But I'm interested in the mistake itself. Foreign anthropologists are always looking to open up things, to reveal things that had been enclosed for centuries.

IJ: Machu Picchu has enormous significance for us, especially through the masterful invocation by Pablo Neruda. Who will not be moved by "Sube a nacer conmigo, hermano," or the English rendition by Nathaniel Tarn, "Arise to birth with me, brother"? Or that incredible crescendo that closes the poem: "Dadme el silencio, el agua, la esperanza. / Dadme la lucha, el hierro, los volcanes. / Apegadme los cuerpos como imanes. / Acudid a mis venas y a mi boca. / Hablad por mis palabras y mi sangre"? Again, in Tarn's translation: "Give me silence, give me water, hope. / Give me the struggle, the iron, the volcanoes. / Let bodies cling like magnets to my body. / Come quickly to my veins and to my mouth. / Speak through my speech, and through my blood." In the tradition of Bello, whom Neruda himself acknowledged as his predecessor in the same endeavor, "Alturas de Macchu Picchu" is a foundational poem that brings past, present, and future together as one glorious continuum in the shaping of the Latin American identity. At the same time, his is a moving voice, a lonely voice that escorts us through history and speaks to us as individuals and as members of a larger community.

IS: I love Neruda's poem on Machu Picchu. Have you been to Machu Picchu?

IJ: No.

IS: I've never visited it either.

IJ: And yet we have both seen the countless images and probably consider it a part of our cultural identity.

IS: It brings to mind José Ortega y Gasset's "Yo soy yo y mi circunstancia"—I am myself and my circumstance.

IJ: I don't doubt, and even hope, that there's something profound in Ortega's dictum. Still, it has always struck me, since my philosophy student days, as an empty notion. It is meant to explain that we are inextricably a part of our surroundings, cultural, social, political, et cetera. This says too much and too little at the same time. It might be peculiar to Spanish culture and philosophy, but in the sad sense that verbosity and tautology are, unfortunately, notorious components of Spanish (and much Spanish American) thought. Still, Ortega was a formidable writer and critic of Spain's situation in the first half of the twentieth century. I'm thinking of his *España invertebrada* (1921).

IS: The Spanish Civil War pushed *casticismo* into an ideology. General Francisco Franco's forces abhorred the Communist threat. That threat was seen as coming from various fronts.

IJ: Yet another instance of how Spain turns on itself to search for that enemy within, in this case the godless, leftist Republicans. What is different about the Civil War is the scale and brutality of the conflict, not unlike our own process of independence.

IS: But I've always been under the impression that the American Civil War was far bloodier than the Wars of Independence in Latin America. The number of casualties exceeds the total of all other U.S. wars combined, from the Revolution to Vietnam. Anyhow, I read that in 2008 a Spanish judge, Baltasar Garzón, issued an order to exhume the remains of the victims of Franquismo buried in nineteen mass graves, including the one believed to contain the remains of Federico García Lorca, the martyred Andalusian poet and one of Neruda's close friends. But his family refused. He had died a horrible death in 1936 under the fascist firing squads. Why unsettle him? the family argued. García Lorca's ordeal—his homosexuality, the use he made of poetry to channel the collective suffering—are emblems of the extremes of *casticismo.*

IJ: The costs of imposing a concept such as this are enormous. By manufacturing otherness, *casticismo* could have this horrendous consequence.

IS: Otherness as threat. One of the best studies of *casticismo* I know of is Luis Buñuel's film *Viridiana,* a reflection on religious mores, sexual desire, and the quest for *beneficencia pública,* a desire to help others. It was a 1961 coproduction between Mexico and Spain and was loosely based on the novel *Halma,* by Benito Pérez Galdós, the ultimate purveyor of *casticismo.* I saw the movie in Mexico in my late teens and have returned to it numerous times. My father acted with Buñuel's actress, Silvia Pinal, in a number of plays. Pinal plays Viridiana, a novitiate who is about to take vows when she visits an uncle on his large estate. He goes wild with her beauty and tries to seduce her but, failing to do so, rapes her while she's asleep. When she finds out, she's outraged and runs away. As a result, her uncle hangs himself. Viridiana turns her mourning into philanthropy: she brings into the estate the local paupers, who go wild one night and take over the building. The scene is superb: Handel's *Messiah* plays in the background as the paupers re-create the scene of Leonardo da Vinci's painting *The Last Supper.* I believe that scene was attacked by the Vatican as heretical, an assessment that generated scandal and brought more attention to the movie. Buñuel's message is clear: when invited to play a role, the lower classes will subvert the system in unforeseen ways. But *Viridiana* is not an anticommunist artifact. Buñuel isn't interested in global politics, at least not in this movie. Instead, he shapes the plot as a meditation on sexual repression that results from a Catholic education. It's obvious at the end that Viridiana cannot return to the convent anymore. In fact, Buñuel suggests a possible ménage à trois with Viridiana as a participant in the concluding scene.

IJ: Buñuel always saw Spanish culture from the outside.

IS: That's why his views are fascinating. *Viridiana* was produced in Spain by the Mexican financier Gustavo Alatriste. The movie is part of Buñuel's Mexican period, in which he did some twenty films, among them *Él, Rehearsal for a Crime* (based on an eponymous novel by playwright Rodolfo Usigli), *Nazarín,* and *The Exterminating Angel.* Buñuel also had a French period. Not only did he draw strength from being an outsider, but it also allowed him to analyze Spanish *casticismo* with lucidity. By the way, I find it telling that, just like Cervantes, García Lorca was an outsider, if not necessarily an outcast, yet his work speaks louder, and deeper, into the wounds of Spain than any other in the same period. Yet let's not turn *casticismo* into a monster. Its pathos includes some daring moments. For instance, do you know that Francisco de Goya's *La maja desnuda* (*The Naked Maja*) has been said to include the first tangible depiction of pubic hair in a Western oil painting? The Greeks enjoyed depicting the human body in naked fashion, but pubic hair is always absent. Of course, Goya also painted *La maja vestida* (*The Clothed Maja*).

IJ: I agree, Spanish art and literature have a strong tradition of dissent, which is often obscured by foreign stereotyping or domestic intolerance. Speaking of Goya, he painted or sketched some of the most compelling images of that critical period during the Napoleonic invasion, when common Spaniards resisted, with rudimentary weapons, the massive French machinery of war. The drawing *Con razón o sin ella* has the air of a nightmare, showing raw anger and the implacable destruction of human life. For what? Goya shows us two sides, the courage of the Spanish people, but at the same time the frightening unleashing of the crudest and most violent expressions of human nature.

IS: By the way, didn't Simón Bolívar unleash a brutality similar to that with his "War to the Death"?

IJ: Yes, although he declared that he would spare those who would join the patriots. It is just a matter of reading the records of the period to see that it was not all that clear. There was horrible brutality on both sides, and the "sides" were constantly changing. Bolívar understood this when he fought for political independence from Spain, but made it clear that he was not too hopeful about the background and virtues of Spanish Americans to lead an independent life. That is why he launched such paternalistic constitutions as the Bolivian charter of 1826 and tried unsuccessfully to introduce the same in Gran Colombia in 1828. He also fought very hard for some sort of supranational union in Spanish America, as exemplified by the Congress of Panama, also in 1826. But he did not set out to fight Spain or unite Latin America on the basis of a concept of hispanidad that added up to more than the desire of Spanish Americans to enjoy the same rights as European Spaniards. No. That was the creation of subsequent leaders, who used Bolívar's emphasis on independence and union as the basis for an emerging sense of Spanish American hispanidad. At first, it was primarily a political construct with some elements of nature and culture, as one can well see in the likes of Bello and Domingo Faustino Sarmiento. Later on, a more explicit recognition of racial diversity, and indeed a celebration of it, was incorporated into national and regional mythologies. But, in essence, Bolívar did not start it, whatever his apologists might say.

IS: You seem to be talking about a very mixed legacy.

IJ: And a very complex individual.

IS: What are the sources of Bolivarismo?

IJ: Bolívar said many different things to many different people, so just about every imaginable political position can claim to be based on his words. Well-intentioned people have read into Bolívar's writings and efforts what they have wanted for their countries and for Latin America in general. But Bolivarismo means primarily an ideal of unity, albeit still an unrealized one. This is all good and healthy, but sometimes it has little to do with the historical context in which Bolívar operated. And even less to do with the manipulations and cynical appropriation of his statements and actions by President Hugo Chávez of Venezuela.

IS: At the political level, doesn't Bolívar underscore the feeling of comradeship among Latin American countries?

IJ: There have been traditional links of solidarity and collaboration, such as the Congress of Panama, and the condemnation of Spain by several Spanish American nations when Isabel II invaded the Chincha Islands in Peru in the 1860s. Throughout the twentieth century, there are multiple examples of solidarity and cross-national friendship. It is often forgotten how many Latin American countries condemned the British invasion of the Malvinas/Falklands in 1982 and how they equally condemned the possible participation of the

United States in the attempted overthrow of Chávez quite recently. There are very strong ties indeed, political, economic, and cultural. But we should not exaggerate them, for one can make an equally plausible argument about lack of unity on many issues.

IS: How about comradeship among people of different countries?

IJ: As we both discovered when we moved to the United States, it is very strong. We may have our differences and our antagonisms, but in the end we all close ranks because we see each other as sharing some very fundamental values and approaches to life.

IS: You seem to be talking about bonds that go beyond nations.

IJ: Yes, although these bonds were forged in a context of confusion and agony. Ever since the expulsion of the Jesuits in 1767, Creole resentments against the Spanish Empire translated into an ambiguous sense of patriotism. "Love of country" could be a double-edged sword. By celebrating the beauty and richness of the continent, and the loyalty of its inhabitants, Creoles were also criticizing the alleged dilapidations of the colonial regime. If one reads Juan Egaña's "Discurso sobre el amor de la patria" (1807), one is struck by this ambivalence. It appears to be a celebration of the empire while at the same time a veiled promotion of independence. But Creoles were also paralyzed by fear, sitting on top of a social scale where they felt caught between the arbitrariness and incompetence of the empire on the one hand, and, on the other, the potential destructiveness of a popular uprising if the colonial government should collapse. When the war started, Spanish Americans began the difficult process of figuring out what was Spanish and what was local and regional in their cultural and political identity.

IS: A most intriguing artifact is Simón Bolívar's "Jamaica Letter," written in 1815 and serving as a political platform for the shaping of an American identity. By then the first domino in what became the quest for independence in the Americas had begun to fall. Mexico was among the first to start that quest, as the priests Miguel Hidalgo y Costilla and José María Morelos y Pavón defied the Spanish rule in New Spain (as Mexico was known at the time), asking the population to subvert the status quo.

IJ: Yes, Bolívar's "Jamaica Letter" is an intriguing and remarkable document. It states that Spanish Americans are neither Europeans, nor Indians, nor Africans, but a peculiar race combining all three. Although he tips the scales heavily against the Spanish side, for propaganda purposes (he is mobilizing for war), he truly means to obliterate Spain as a presence in Latin America. He sees nothing but oppression and decadence in the second-rate Spanish Empire. At the same time, he did not quite rely on any sense of Spanish American political identity for the construction of new nations, because he strongly believed that the population lacked political virtue. There had to be a process of political de-Hispanization first and foremost, while at the same time avoiding any sort of indigenous political construct. Laws and political philosophy had to be European, but republican institutions had to be adapted to the peculiar racial, social, and geographical makeup of the region. Minus Spain.

IS: I'm fascinated by the concept you're expounding: Bolívar's belief that the first step toward the creation of a continental identity in the Americas was de-Hispanization—that is, a rejection of Spain as the principal source of political and cultural sustenance. I'm attracted to the concept because it suggests that la hispanidad has a reverse side and that, in the Spanish colonies, it required a redefinition that, at its heart, would extricate Spain from it. Nowadays the tendency is to perceive the Hispanic world as oscillating between two poles: Spain and the Americas. But in the early part of the nineteenth century, the Americas, in order to set themselves free from oppression, rejected the other pole as unnecessary, even redundant.

IJ: Keep in mind, Ilan, that when Bolívar drafted the "Jamaica Letter," Spain was perceived, not only on this side of the Atlantic but also in Europe, as an awkward country really out of sync with contemporary political realities.

IS: Not only awkward but obscurantist. It was a response to the imperial decline. Other empires (the Romans, Byzantium, the Portuguese, the British) have gone through a similar state of internal depression. The process culminated with the war of 1898, when Spain lost control of its remaining colonies in the Caribbean and the Pacific, and the United States emerged as an indisputable hemispheric power. By the way, what was the precise circumstance that pushed Bolívar to write the "Jamaica Letter"?

IJ: In 1815 he realized that his military reconquest of Venezuela during the Campaña Admirable, or Admirable Campaign, had meant little or nothing to the "people" he had in mind to liberate from Spanish oppression. He was essentially defeated by the *llaneros* (cowboys of the plains) who had sided with the royalists. He was deeply conflicted, but he learned his lesson: without capturing the hearts and minds of those very same *llaneros,* he would not win. He also realized that he needed international support, and saw England as the only likely candidate, on account of British interest in commerce in the region. So in the Jamaica letter, addressed to a "British gentleman," he mixes all kinds of arguments to reflect on the realities of the war, the nature of the population, and the rather unrealistic political and economic prospects of the region, in order to appeal to British intervention on behalf of his independence project. He was sadly disappointed, but he did provide a blueprint in this letter for what needed to happen to make independence possible. This letter also marks an important personal transition for Bolívar: he was no longer reacting to events. From now on he was to become an independence fighter on all fronts. It is really impressive how he was able to plan his next moves even from the depths of defeat.

IS: An important element of Bolívar's thinking was his belief in unity, which is still quite appealing.

IJ: You state in *The Hispanic Condition* (1995) that it is ironic that Bolívar's *ideario,* his political dream of unification of a great portion of South America (and Panama) in a nation he envisioned as Gran Colombia, came to nothing, as a result of overwhelming socioeconomic and political realities. And yet, at the beginning of the twenty-first century, that *ideario* is alive and well, with important differences, in the United States, where a forty-million-plus Latino community has emerged as a powerful minority.

IS: Through a cumbersome mutation, la hispanidad becomes *la latinidad* in the United States. Among other reasons, this is because a minority has a particular idiosyncrasy that differs from the behavior of a nation or a regional alliance. But before we delve into the topic, I want to explore further the intellectual atmosphere in which Bolívar allowed the concept of la hispanidad to gestate in the former colonies.

IJ: Let me try. Ever since the expulsion of the Jesuits in the 1760s, Spanish Americans were painfully aware of the unwelcome demands placed upon them by a rejuvenated empire under Charles III. But they were also painfully aware that they lived in a divided society and that Creoles in particular had much to lose should there be a rebellion of slaves and *castas*. So they were caught on the horns of a dilemma: how to advance their interests, which the empire denied, without stirring up a hornets' nest, which they feared more than the absolutism of the late Bourbons. Much of the significant political thinking of the time didn't put it this way, but you can see in the various documents a mix of fake obedience and resentment, as well as a deep distrust and indeed fear of popular rebellions. Latin American Creoles oscillated between the two poles, but in the end they realized that with an empire overrun by Napoléon, they were the best custodians of their own interests, which meant protecting their social and economic position. They fought for independence not so much against a feeble Spain as against their own subjects, until eventually they crossed that Rubicon of mobilizing their subjects against the empire. Otherwise, independence would not have happened.

IS: It might be suitable to reflect, at this point, on the varied feelings that the intelligentsia in the Americas had in the early part of the nineteenth century regarding hemispheric unity and, more concretely, about la hispanidad. Andrés Bello, for instance.

IJ: Bello was really quite beyond the anti-Spanish passions of Bolívar and the generation that participated in the actual struggle for independence. He thought that Spanish America had to build on the solid foundations of Hispanic traditions. To him, it would be a mistake to confuse one particular period (the colonial period) with the entire history of Hispanic civilization, which had to be traced to Roman times. He had specific reasons in mind: in order to build republics based on the rule of law, there had to be a legislation that made sense. What made sense was the Roman origin of Iberian law, which by the way was still in place, and he thought that the new republics had to build from there. Incorporate, not reject, was his motto. At the same time, there were some less practical, more philosophical reasons: he was interested in order, and order could be sustained only if it was firmly rooted in the traditions of the past. He believed that Spanish America would be in a stronger position if it looked past the animosities of the independence period and rediscovered in Spain the sources of its language and culture.

IS: And yet Bello is often celebrated as the founder of an early Creole sense of Spanish American identity.

IJ: Rightly so, though his inclination to cultural continuity did not preclude a very strong Americanismo, as when he addressed "Poetry" in 1823, just as the wars of independence were reaching their climax:

> Divina Poesía,
> Tú de la soledad habitadora,
> A consultar tus cantos enseñada
> Con el silencio de la selva umbría,
> Tú a quien la verde gruta fue morada,
> Y el eco de los montes compañía;
> Tiempo es que dejes ya la culta Europa,
> Que tu nativa rustiquez desama,
> Y dirijas el vuelo donde te abre
> El mundo de Colón su grande escena.

In the translation of Frances López-Morillas:

> Divine poetry,
> You who dwell in solitude
> Taught to enwrap your songs
> In the shady forest's silence,
> You who lived in the green grotto
> And had for company the mountain's echo;
> It is time for you to leave effete Europe,
> No lover of your native rustic charms,
> And fly to where Columbus's world
> Opens its great scene before your eyes.

He did not wait for others to answer the call, and in his "Ode to Tropical Agriculture" (1826), written in London, he bequeathed to posterity a celebration of the scenery, resources, and promise of Spanish America:

> ¡Salve, fecunda zona,
> que al sol enamorado circunscribes
> el vago curso, y cuanto ser se anima
> en cada vario clima,
> acariciada de su luz, concibes!

And in the translation of Frances López-Morillas:

Hail, fertile zone, that circumscribes
The errant course of your enamored sun,
And, caressed by its light,
Brings forth all living things
In each of your many climes!

Bello's verses rhyme with sugarcane, chocolate, and cactus, and sing of the yucca, the potato, the banana, and the pineapple. No wonder Miguel Ángel Asturias admired his local themes and references, and Neruda said that Bello started his *Canto general* before he did. Bello is certainly among the best-known poets celebrating Spanish American themes, much like Longfellow in the United States at about the same time.

IS: Another important figure of the time who made a contribution to the concept of la hispanidad, even as an opponent of Bello, is Domingo Faustino Sarmiento. He was in many ways opposed to the Venezuelan's view of American unity. From his various books, the one with a solid claim to immortality, in spite of Sarmiento's own original intentions, is *Facundo* (1845). The subtitle is emblematic and at times has eclipsed the title itself: *Civilization and Barbarism.*

IJ: You wrote the introduction to the 1998 Penguin edition of *Facundo.*

IS: The publisher wanted to use *Civilization and Barbarism* alone on the cover. The reason is simply this: Sarmiento struck a chord when he suggested that Argentina, and by synecdoche the Americas, ought to be seen as a field where the forces of order and chaos are in constant battle. Granted, it sometimes feels that way. Looking at the region through that prism complicates the concept of la hispanidad. It might suggest a dream of unity, but it also defines the society that nurtures it as volatile.

IJ: That's an extrapolation that Sarmiento didn't necessarily make . . .

IS: I agree. Yet in his 1845 portrait of his gaucho protagonist, Juan Facundo Quiroga, which Sarmiento wrote while in exile in Santiago, he offered a vision of what Argentina ought to be as an independent nation. In his eyes the gaucho, as a social type, was dangerous. Sarmiento wanted the Argentine landscape to be at once more urban and more European. To this effect, he was in favor of Italian and other European immigration to the country. What I mean to say is that Sarmiento's view of la hispanidad did not endorse Spain, but it certainly embraced Europe as a model. But surely he was aware that other people had different views on both Spain and la hispanidad, as Bello did.

IJ: Yes, Sarmiento collaborated with Bello on some issues, particularly the spelling reforms of the 1840s, and shared his sense of the importance of educated journalism, but they were on opposite ends of the cultural and political spectrum. Sarmiento was rabidly anti-Spanish, a bias he reinforced when he visited the country during the second half of the 1840s. *Facundo* is in some ways a proposal for liberal political development, but it is also a strong condemnation of anything Spanish. Like the U.S. Hispanists writing at about the same time, he viewed Spain as the home of despotism and religious intolerance. Nothing good could come out of it. Although Facundo Quiroga was depicted as a sort of primeval barbarian, Sarmiento viewed him and the people of his kind as the products of the colonial legacy. Just as they sought to destroy (liberal) civilization, they had to be destroyed for the sake of it.

IS: Whenever I think of *Facundo,* my mind invokes another Latin American foundational book. This one is from Brazil and was published in the early days of the twentieth century: *Os Sertões,* by Euclides da Cunha. I recently looked at Elizabeth Lowe's new English translation. Like Sarmiento's treatise, it is a racist, xenophobic narrative addressing the uprising of *jagunços,* the dwellers of the backlands in Canudos, in the state of Bahia, whose leader, Antônio Conselheiro, was described by the media of the time as a religious fanatic. In many ways, Cunha's book is about nation building. Or better, about nation destruction.

IJ: You are referring to the Canudos rebellion, which took place in 1896 and 1897.

IS: Brazil, as you know, had a false start in regards to its independence. Although it ceased its connection to Portugal in 1822, more or less when other emerging nations in the continent were cutting their umbilical cord with Spain, it wasn't until 1888 that slavery was abolished, and 1889 that the country became a republic. The Canudos campaign, in which the government sent military forces to quiet the *jagunços,* was seen as essential to keep the republic intact. Indeed,

Cunha in 1897 wrote a couple of articles for the daily newspaper *O Estado de São Paulo* called "A nossa Vendéia." In them he related Canudos to Vendée, the region in west-central France on the Atlantic Ocean, where in 1793 a peasant revolt against the newly formed revolutionary government took place, hoping to reestablish the monarch that had been brought down a few years prior. To suppress Conselheiro and his hoodlums, thus, was a way to show the world that Brazil was a true modern nation. But to achieve the goal, between ten thousand and twenty thousand people had to die.

What I like about *Os Sertões* is the way it addresses urgent questions that affect us today. It is, in essence, a report on war. For about a month Cunha was in Canudos, where he witnessed the atrocities. He may present the *jagunços* as barbarians, but his portrait of the government isn't much better. He described the army as made of brutes. It is interesting to note that another U.S. Hispanist, Samuel Putnam, who also translated Cervantes's *Exemplary Novels* and *Don Quixote* and is the father of philosopher Hilary Putnam, lucidly translated the book for the University of Chicago Press. It came out in 1944, just as World War II was reaching its final stage and the Holocaust was beginning to be known at the global level.

By the way, I'm attracted to Sarmiento's travels through the United States.

IJ: He was mesmerized by the United States, particularly the educational policies of some states, which he thought to be the best in the world. He was thinking primarily of those introduced by Horace Mann, whom he interviewed in West Newton, Massachusetts, in 1847. His trip was short and his study of U.S. institutions not very deep. But he became a convert. Everything Hispanic was bad; everything American was good. His later trip in the 1860s, now as ambassador of Argentina, was more sober (it was in the aftermath of the Civil War, after all), but he was still a staunch admirer. He used this second stay on American soil primarily to promote himself as an intellectual and also to establish the foundations of his political campaign for the presidency of Argentina, which he won in 1868. He was a pro-American liberal with a strong bias against la hispanidad.

IS: Equally important is Sarmiento's relationship with his translator—and his publicity agent—Mary Mann, the widow of New England pedagogue Horace Mann.

IJ: Oh, yes! He had her translate *Facundo* into English, which became for a long time the text that generations of Americans used to view Spanish American political culture. Although he manipulated her for his own advancement and political purposes, she was no passive, wide-eyed fan. She had her own agenda, which was to promote the educational philosophy of her late husband. If Sarmiento could implement those ideas on a national level in Argentina, she would have a strong claim to advance those very same views in Reconstruction America. That is the central reason why she collaborated with Sarmiento, but her impact went quite beyond it: her translation had an enormous influence on the way Americans viewed the Hispanic world.

IS: She is a good example of how a translator can also be an agitator.

IJ: I know she struggled to understand and translate Sarmiento's hyperbole and impenetrable idiomatic expressions. For many years I used her translation in my teaching, which you also used in the Penguin edition. But I must ask, in this context, what was your sense of her work? She was suddenly confronted with a world she had no idea about, and yet had to put words into experiences and places she did not know.

IS: That, in my eyes, is exactly the challenge that translators face in their work: to make an unknown world come alive. Indeed, Mary Mann's paradigm might be the perfect example. What about José Victorino Lastarria?

IJ: Lastarria was a young disciple of Andrés Bello. But like many disciples seeking to establish their intellectual independence, he built a case against his mentor's alleged conservatism. He first challenged Bello's request, as rector of the newly founded University of Chile (1842), that he present the inaugural historical paper before the fully assembled faculty, in accordance with the rules of the university's statutes. The paper had to be based on documentary evidence, so as to provide the foundations and the tone of Chilean historiography. Lastarria chose to write about the impact of colonial rule on current Chilean institutions and customs. It was an incendiary pamphlet, denouncing the colonial period as a cruel winter three centuries long. Nothing good had come out of it, Lastarria stated, and the trouble was that the colonial legacy persisted in the form of authoritarian political practices and the influence of the Catholic Church. This argument became a major issue, not just because the University of Chile was a state institution and Catholicism was the constitutionally recognized religion of the country, but also because it was clearly a violation of the university's statutes: the paper was based not on impartial evidence but on the model of the eighteenth-century "philosophy of history," which set out to study the past in order to change the present. This invited a most interesting polemic on the purposes of history, which is among the intellectual gems of our cultural history. But what most people retained at the time—and beyond—was the acrimonious anti-Spanish sentiment. It is not coincidence that, at exactly the same time, the Chilean government was negotiating the Spanish recognition of independence, which was finally achieved in 1844. The opposition to the government, to which Lastarria belonged, was against seeking political legitimacy from Spain. In essence, Lastarria and others (including Francisco Bilbao) are representative of a time when anti-Spanish ideology with strongly anti-Catholic undertones was still seen as the foundation for national political identity.

IS: We might do well to consider the Mexican experience, for Mexico is a country that has probably had the toughest time incorporating the Spanish conquest into its own independent national history.

IJ: Enduring icons that still persist, such as Moctezuma, Cuauhtémoc, the Malinche, and Hernán Cortés, are just a few examples of the deep impact of the Spanish conquest, and the incentives for Mexican intellectuals and politicians in the post-independence period to develop a fervently anti-Spanish ideology. And yet the picture is surprisingly nuanced. In building their nation, Mexicans did not reject the Spanish past as thoroughly as Lastarria did. What they did do was to value indigenous history, but without rejecting the Spanish heritage. I am talking about leading intellectuals like Lucas Alamán, Carlos María Bustamante, José Fernando Ramírez, José María Luis Mora, and Joaquín García Icazbalceta, the founders of Mexican historiography. Without them, we would know precious little about the Aztecs and previous Mesoamerican civilizations. But we learn much more, insofar as they rescued the indigenous past but were quite paternalistic about contemporary Indians. What is very clear is that they understood that the new Mexican nation could not afford to ignore them. If Mexico was to prosper as an inclusive nation, it had to find a place for its Indians and mestizos. The figure of Hernán Cortés was somewhat more complicated, and there you could see Lucas Alamán and Carlos María Bustamante on opposite sides of the spectrum. Still, the consensus was that the colonial period was not an unmitigated disaster but rather the foundation for what Mexico would become. The more anti-Spanish and *indigenista* versions came after the Mexican Revolution; during this crucial period in the making of a Spanish American hispanidad, Mexico showed a clear tendency toward reconciliation with Spain and its past in the Americas.

IS: A new age came along at the end of the nineteenth century. In his book *The Lettered City* (1984), the Uruguayan critic Ángel Rama talked about the arrival of electricity as well as potable water, the cinematograph, and the telegraph as technological devices that changed forever the Latin American metropolis.

IJ: Yes, indeed, but let us keep in mind that the purpose of Rama's book is to talk about the resilience and survival of a class of *letrados* who, since colonial times, had put their talents to the service of the state in exchange for patronage and a position of unparalleled influence. He views intellectuals as chameleons who adjust to whatever is expected of them from the true sources of power. We might disagree with this view, and I am one among them, but Rama is absolutely right that at least some intellectuals jumped eagerly onto the bandwagon of modernity to promote the specific development policies of various regimes, in particular Mexico and Argentina, which are the national cases he mentioned the most in this regard.

IS: It was the age known as *modernismo.* The term ought not to be confused with its English equivalent, modernism, an aesthetic movement that included figures like James Joyce, Virginia Woolf, Ernest Hemingway, Scott Fitzgerald, and so on. The *modernistas,* it might be said, were the ones responsible for spreading the gospel of la hispanidad. José Martí, Rubén Darío, Julián del Casal, José Asunción Silva, Ricardo Jaimes Freyre, Amado Nervo, Enrique González Martínez, Delmira Agustini, and Leopoldo Lugones, among others, were part of the first aesthetic movement in the Americas to look at the region as a whole. Surely, they were infatuated with French culture (Parnassianism, Symbolism, etc.), and a few of them, like Darío, used the French mode to deliver their message. But their political viewpoint was far more sophisticated. As a journalist in New York, Martí wrote some of the most inspired essays about the United States, but since his audience was in Mexico City and Buenos Aires, he needed to create a rhetorical style that, as it turns out, emphasized his view on *nuestra América:* a language for anyone in the Spanish-speaking Americas.

IJ: What works come to mind?

IS: I'm thinking of Darío's mannered poems like "Los cisnes" (The Swans), published in 1905 and dedicated to Juan Ramón Jiménez.

> ¿Qué signo haces, oh Cisne, con tu encorvado cuello
> al paso de los tristes y errantes soñadores?
> ¿Por qué tan silencioso de ser blanco y ser bello,
> tiránico a las aguas e impasible a las flores?
>
> Yo te saludo ahora como en versos latinos
> te saludara antaño Publio Ovidio Nasón.
> Los mismos ruiseñores cantan los mismos trinos,
> y en diferentes lenguas es la misma canción.
>
> A vosotros mi lengua no debe ser extraña.
> A Garcilaso visteis, acaso, alguna vez...
> Soy un hijo de América, soy un nieto de España...
> Quevedo pudo hablaros en verso en Aranjuez....
>
> Cisnes, los abanicos de vuestras alas frescas
> den a las frentes pálidas sus caricias más puras
> y alejen vuestras blancas figuras pintorescas
> de nuestras mentes tristes las ideas obscuras.
>
> Brumas septentrionales nos llenan de tristezas,
> se mueren nuestras rosas, se agostan nuestras palmas,
> casi no hay ilusiones para nuestras cabezas,
> y somos los mendigos de nuestras pobres almas.
>
> Nos predican la guerra con águilas feroces,
> gerifaltes de antaño revienen a los puños,
> mas no brillan las glorias de las antiguas hoces,
> ni hay Rodrigos ni Jaimes, ni hay Alfonsos ni Nuños.

Faltos del alimento que dan las grandes cosas,
¿qué haremos los poetas sino buscar tus lagos?
A falta de laureles son muy dulces las rosas,
y a falta de victorias busquemos los halagos.

La América Española como la España entera
fija está en el Oriente de su fatal destino;
yo interrogo a la Esfinge que el porvenir espera
con la interrogación de tu cuello divino.

¿Seremos entregados a los bárbaros fieros?
¿Tantos millones de hombres hablaremos inglés?
¿Ya no hay nobles hidalgos ni bravos caballeros?
¿Callaremos ahora para llorar después?

He lanzado mi grito, Cisnes, entre vosotros,
que habéis sido los fieles en la desilusión,
mientras siento una fuga de americanos potros
y el estertor postrero de un caduco león...

...Y un Cisne negro dijo: "La noche anuncia el día."
Y uno blanco: "¡La aurora es inmortal, la aurora
es inmortal!" ¡Oh tierras de sol y de armonía,
aún guarda la Esperanza la caja de Pandora!

The translation into English, by Greg Simon and Steven F. White, of the crucial quartet:

Are we to be overrun by the cruel barbarians?
Is it our fate that millions of us will speak in English?
Are there no fierce shining knights, no valiant noblemen?
Shall we keep our silence now, to weep later in anguish?

The swan, of course, was Darío's favorite symbol...

IJ: The references that appear to be about the United States, like "ferocious eagles" and "cruel barbarians," are striking. Do you sense a mix of rejection and admiration for the country on the part of Darío?

IS: Let me illustrate this with Darío's medallion to Roosevelt, which is among the most radical of *modernista* poems. It was published in 1904.

¡Es con voz de la Biblia, o verso de Walt Whitman,
que habría que llegar hasta ti, Cazador!
¡Primitivo y moderno, sencillo y complicado,
con un algo de Washington y cuatro de Nemrod!
Eres los Estados Unidos,
eres el futuro invasor
de la América ingenua que tiene sangre indígena,
que aún reza a Jesucristo y aún habla en español.

Eres soberbio y fuerte ejemplar de tu raza;
eres culto, eres hábil; te opones a Tolstoy.
Y domando caballos, o asesinando tigres,
eres un Alejandro-Nabucodonosor.
(Eres un profesor de energía,
como dicen los locos de hoy.)
Crees que la vida es incendio,
que el progreso es erupción;
en donde pones la bala
el porvenir pones.

               No.

Los Estados Unidos son potentes y grandes.
Cuando ellos se estremecen hay un hondo temblor
que pasa por las vértebras enormes de los Andes.
Si clamáis, se oye como el rugir del león.
Ya Hugo a Grant le dijo: "Las estrellas son vuestras."
(Apenas brilla, alzándose, el argentino sol
y la estrella chilena se levanta . . .) Sois ricos.
Juntáis al culto de Hércules el culto de Mammón;
y alumbrando el camino de la fácil conquista,
la Libertad levanta su antorcha en Nueva York.

Mas la América nuestra, que tenía poetas
desde los viejos tiempos de Netzahualcoyotl,
que ha guardado las huellas de los pies del gran Baco,
que el alfabeto pánico en un tiempo aprendió;
que consultó los astros, que conoció la Atlántida,
cuyo nombre nos llega resonando en Platón,
que desde los remotos momentos de su vida

vive de luz, de fuego, de perfume, de amor,
la América del gran Moctezuma, del Inca,
la América fragante de Cristóbal Colón,
la América católica, la América española,
la América en que dijo el noble Guatemoc:
"Yo no estoy en un lecho de rosas"; esa América
que tiembla de huracanes y que vive de Amor,
hombres de ojos sajones y alma bárbara, vive.
Y sueña. Y ama, y vibra; y es la hija del Sol.
Tened cuidado. ¡Vive la América española!
Hay mil cachorros sueltos del León Español.
Se necesitaría, Roosevelt, ser Dios mismo,
el Riflero terrible y el fuerte Cazador,
para poder tenernos en vuestras férreas garras.

Y, pues contáis con todo, falta una cosa: ¡Dios!

Herein a translation—or better, an adaptation—into English, also
by Greg Simon and Steven F. White:

The voice of the Bible, or a stanza by Walt Whitman—
isn't that what it would take to reach your ears, Great Hunter?
You're primitive and modern, simple and complicated,
made of one part Washington and perhaps four parts Nimrod!
You yourself are the United States.
You will be a future invader
of naïve America, the one with Indian blood,
that still prays to Jesus Christ and still speaks the Spanish tongue.

You're arrogant and you're strong, exemplary of your race;
you're cultivated, you're skilled, you stand opposed to Tolstoy.
You're a tamer of horses, you're a killer of tigers,
you're like some Alexander mixed with Nebuchadnezzar.
(You must be the Energy Professor
as the crazies today might put it)

You think that life is one big fire,
that progress is just eruption,
that wherever you put bullets,
you put the future, too.
                    No.

The U.S. is a country that is powerful and strong.
When the giant yawns and stretches, the earth feels a tremor
rippling through the enormous vertebrae of the Andes.
If you shout, the sound you make is a lion's roar.
Hugo once said this to Grant: "You possess the stars."
(The Argentine sun at dawn gives off hardly any light;
and the Chilean star is rising higher . . .) You're so rich,
you join the cult to Hercules with the cult to Mammon.
And lighting the broad straight path that leads to easy conquests,
Lady Liberty raises her torch in New York City.

But our own America, which had plenty of poets
even from the ancient times of Netzahualcoyotl,
and which retained the footprints from the feet of Great Bacchus,
and, over the course of time, learned the Panic alphabet:
it sought advice from the stars, and knew of Atlantis,
whose name was a legacy, resonating in Plato.
Even from the most remote moments in its boundless life,
it has lived by light and fire, by fragrances and by love:
America of the great Moctezuma and Inca,
America redolent of Christopher Columbus,
Catholic America and Spanish America,
the place where once long ago the noble Cuátemoc said,
"I'm not on a bed of roses!" Yes, that America,
trembling from its hurricanes and surviving on its Love . . .
It lives with you, with your Saxon eyes and barbaric souls.
And dreams. And loves, and vibrates; it's the daughter of
      the Sun.
Be careful. Spanish America is alive and well!
There are myriad loose cubs now from the Spanish Lion.
Roosevelt, you'd need to be transfigured by God himself
into the dire Rifleman and the powerful Hunter
to finally capture us in your talons of iron.

And you think you have it all, but one thing is missing: God!

IJ: You wrote about it in the introduction to the Penguin Classics
edition *Selected Writings: Rubén Darío* (2005). How do you read his
position regarding the United States?

IS: The "no" at the heart of the medallion is an accusation that the United States, under a veil of pretended camaraderie, usurps its neighbor's space and freedom.

IJ: Do you see the same charge coming from other contemporary intellectuals?

IS: Perhaps even more than Darío, José Martí, principally through the dispatches he sent to newspapers like Buenos Aires's *La Nación* from his exile in the United States. There he offered a portrait of Hispanic civilization in ways I would describe as a Popperian "negative attribute."

IJ: Can you mention an example?

IS: Think of his essay "Our America." The essay explores the concept of la hispanidad as a call to unity.

> De todos sus peligros se va salvando América. Sobre algunas repúblicas está durmiendo el pulpo. Otras, por la ley del equilibrio, se echan a pie a la mar, a recobrar, con prisa loca y sublime, los siglos perdidos. Otras, olvidando que Juárez paseaba en un coche de mulas, ponen coche de viento y de cochero a una bomba de jabón; el lujo venenoso, enemigo de la libertad, pudre al hombre liviano y abre la puerta al extranjero. Otras acendran, con el espíritu épico de la independencia amenazada, el carácter viril. Otras crían, en la guerra rapaz contra el vecino, la soldadesca que puede devorarlas. Pero otro peligro corre, acaso, nuestra América, que no le viene de sí, sino de la diferencia de orígenes, métodos e intereses entre los dos factores continentales, y es la hora próxima en que se le acerque demandando relaciones íntimas, un pueblo emprendedor y pujante que la desconoce y la desdeña. Y como los pueblos viriles, que se han hecho de sí propios, con la escopeta y la ley, aman, y sólo aman, a los pueblos viriles; como la hora del desenfreno y la ambición, de que acaso se libre, por el predominio de lo más puro de su sangre, la América del Norte, o el que pudieran lanzarla sus masas vengativas y sórdidas, la tradición de conquista y el interés de un caudillo hábil, no está tan cercana aún a los ojos del más espantadizo, que no dé tiempo a la prueba de altivez, continua y discreta, con que se la pudiera encarar y desviarla; como su decoro de república pone a la América del Norte, ante los pueblos atentos del Universo, un freno que no le ha de quitar la provocación pueril o la arrogancia ostentosa, o la discordia parricida de nuestra América, el deber urgente de nuestra América es ense-

ñarse como es, una en alma e intento, vencedora veloz de un pasado sofocante, manchada sólo con sangre de abono que arranca a las manos la pelea con las ruinas, y la de las venas que nos dejaron picadas nuestros dueños. El desdén del vecino formidable, que no la conoce, es el peligro mayor de nuestra América; y urge, porque el día de la visita está próximo, que el vecino la conozca, la conozca pronto, para que no la desdeñe. Por ignorancia llegaría, tal vez, a poner en ella la codicia. Por el respeto, luego que la conociese, sacaría de ella las manos. Se ha de tener fe en lo mejor del hombre y desconfiar de lo peor de él. Hay que dar ocasión a lo mejor para que se revele y prevalezca sobre lo peor. Si no, lo peor prevalece. Los pueblos han de tener una picota para quien les azuza a odios inútiles; y otra para quien no les dice a tiempo la verdad.

A translation by Esther Allen:

America is escaping all its dangers. Some of the republics are still beneath the sleeping octopus, but others, under the law of averages, are draining their land with sublime and furious haste, as if to make up for centuries lost. Still others, forgetting that Juarez went about in a carriage drawn by mules, hitch their carriages to the wind, their coachmen soap bubbles. Poisonous luxury, the enemy of freedom, corrupts the frivolous and opens the door to the foreigner. In others, where independence is threatened, an epic spirit heightens their manhood. Still others spawn an army capable of devouring them in voracious wars. But perhaps our America is running another risk that does not come from itself but from the difference in origins, methods, and interests between the two halves of the continent, and the time is near at hand when an enterprising and vigorous people who scorn and ignore our America will even so approach it and demand a close relationship. And since strong nations, self-made by law and shotgun, love strong nations and them alone; since the time of madness and ambition—from which North America may be freed by the predominance of the purest elements in its blood, or on which it may be launched by its vindictive and sordid masses, its tradition of expansion, or the ambition of some powerful leader—is not so near at hand, even to the most timorous eye, that there is no time for the test of discreet and unwavering pride that could confront and dissuade it; since its good name as a republic in the eyes of the world's perceptive nations puts upon North America a restraint that cannot be taken away by childish provocations or pompous arrogance or parricidal discords among our American nations— the pressing need of our America is to show itself as it is, one in spirit and intent, swift conquerors of a suffocating past, stained only by the enriching blood drawn from the scars left upon us by our masters. The scorn of our formidable neighbor who does not know us is our America's greatest danger. And since the day of the visit is near, it is imperative that our neighbor know us, and soon, so that it will not scorn us. Through ignorance it might even come to lay hands on us. Once it does know us, it will remove its hands out of respect. One must have faith in the best in men and distrust the worst. One must allow the best to be shown so that it reveals and prevails over the worst. Nations should have a pillory for whoever stirs up useless hate, and another for whoever fails to tell them the truth in time.

IJ: Truly a call for unity, but quite denunciatory of the United States.

IS: There is also Martí's poem about the two Cubas. It's called "Dos patrias," in English "Two Homelands."

Dos patrias tengo yo: Cuba y la noche
¿O son una las dos? No bien retira
su majestad el sol, con largos velos
Y un clavel en la mano, silenciosa
Cuba cual viuda triste me aparece.
¡Yo sé cuál es ese clavel sangriento
Que en la mano le tiembla! Está vacío
Mi pecho, destrozado está y vacío
Donde estaba el corazón. Ya es hora
De empezar a morir. La noche es buena
Para decir adiós. La luz estorba
Y la palabra humana. El universo
Habla mejor que el hombre.
    Cual bandera
que invita a batallar, la llama roja

de la vela flamea. Las ventanas
abro, ya estrecho en mí. Muda, rompiendo
las hojas del clavel, como una nube
que enturbia el cielo, Cuba, viuda, pasa.

Herein my own English version:

I have two homelands: Cuba and the night.
Or are they one and the same? No sooner
does his majesty, the sun, retire, than Cuba, with long veils,
and a carnation in hand, silently,
like a sad widow, appears before me.
I know that bleeding carnation
trembling in her hand! It's empty,
my chest is destroyed and empty
where the heart once was. It's time
to begin dying. The night is
the right time to say good-bye. The light is bothersome
and so are human words. The universe
speaks better than man.
          Like a flag
inviting us to battle, the candle's
red flame flickers. Too full of myself,
I open the windows. Silent, plucking
the carnation's leaves, like a cloud
darkening the sky, Cuba, like a widow, passes by.

Martí suggests a homeland—*his* homeland—divided. The division, in his eyes, is like a widow mourning her children.

IJ: It also seems to be a call for struggle, "cual bandera / que invita a batallar." Could he have predicted that the struggle against Spain would lead to U.S. occupation?

IS: Perhaps not. He was more focused on the immediate struggle at hand. But arguably, no war has ever defined the Hispanic world as a whole the way the Spanish-American War of 1898 did.

IJ: And yet the war of 1898 is the culmination of a process that began with the Mexican-American War of 1846–1848: the relentless expansion of the United States into former Spanish territory, with the attendant arrogance of all conquerors. The last quarter of the nineteenth century is the time of a toxic combination of Manifest Destiny ideology and various purportedly "scientific" theories on race. Everything Hispanic became synonymous with indolence, laziness, inferiority. The pioneers of Hispanic studies in the United States stressed the legacies of the Spanish Empire, mainly slavery, religious intolerance, and despotism. But with the Spanish-American War we see the unabashed racist characterization of everything Hispanic. No wonder, then, that José Enrique Rodó, two years later, would respond with his *Ariel,* to denounce the expansionism of the United States and to counter its implications with a more positive view of the Hispanic world.

IS: Would you say that Rodó added a new component to the notion of la hispanidad?

IJ: As we discussed before, some nineteenth-century liberals tried to de-Hispanize Latin America by connecting it to wider intellectual and economic trends in the developed world. Positivists accelerated the process, but then the shock came, bluntly, in the form of a United States that had done much to modernize, yet accompanied this process with territorial expansion, imperialism, and the denigration of Hispanic culture. One must see Rodó's *Ariel* in that context, which culminated with the Spanish-American War of 1898 and led to the takeover of Cuba and Puerto Rico. Rodó was not exactly a diehard conservative who tried to return to the roots of a traditional Hispanic culture, or a rabidly anti-American nationalist, but rather a humanist who denounced the consequences of the conflict by pointing to the dangers of modernity when deprived of a spiritual inspiration. He thought that the United States had reached the point of modernity without spirit and that Latin America should not follow that path, which he acknowledged to be tempting. Instead, Latin America ought to develop a spiritual, aesthetic life that would counter the detrimental effects of materialism, utilitarianism, and democracy. "We imitate what we believe to be superior or prestigious," he warned. "And this is why the vision of an America de-Latinized of its own will, without threat of conquest, and reconstituted in the image and likeness of the North, now looms in the nightmares of many who are genuinely concerned about our future" (Margaret Sayers Peden's translation). Note the use of the word "de-Latinized," where *Latin* means the spiritual and the aesthetic represented by Ariel. All of this is idealized, but in the context of the time it stands as a valiant effort to resist the denigration and impoverishment of Hispanic cultures, and an assertion of the humanistic values that provide the basis for a new sense of cultural identity, which future generations of Spanish Americans would seek to establish.

SPREADING THE
YANKEE GOSPEL

IVÁN JAKSIĆ: You've talked about *la latinidad* as a concept developed in the United States, although, as you pointed out, with some European origins. Let's focus on U.S. conceptions of the Hispanic world.

ILAN STAVANS: In the Americas, la hispanidad cannot be separated from the view of Hispanic culture within the United States.

IJ: Truly, not only because some Americans developed early views on Hispanic culture, often in dialogue with nationals in Spain and in Latin America, but also because Hispanics have steadily made their presence known in the United States. They have developed notions of identity that are part of the collective experience of Hispanics everywhere.

IS: You've studied what I once described as "the unMetaphysical Club," a cadre of New Englanders in the nineteenth century whose interest in the Hispanic world was, to a large extent, a response to the anemic Spanish Empire that ultimately collapsed in the war of 1898. How did you decide to embark on this journey?

IJ: I stumbled upon that group during my research on Andrés Bello, who knew their work and at times had direct contact with them. They are really quite a remarkable group. I refer to George Ticknor, Henry W. Longfellow, Mary Peabody Mann, William H. Prescott, and Washington Irving. They are now mostly forgotten, in large part because their scholarship has been superseded or their style of writing no longer resonates. But they made a fundamental contribution to American intellectual life and national identity by defining what the United States should not do, to avoid decline and collapse. And they found a most convenient example in the case of the Spanish Empire. Everything they disliked they found in Spain and, by extension, Spanish America: a marked tendency toward despotism and religious intolerance. Also, they found in Spain a convenient way to avoid the central dilemmas posed by slavery. They blamed its introduction on Spain and argued that there was an even worse form of slavery, that represented by the Inquisition and the Catholic Church: the slavery of the mind. At the same time, they could be quite progressive, in that they warned the United States about the danger of its own imperial ambitions, which they saw firsthand in the invasion of Mexico in 1846. They believed that the invasion was a clear sign that their country had entered that fatal cycle in the life of nations, the moment when they become empires and enter the successive and inevitable stages of decline and collapse.

IS: How did Washington Irving discover Hispanic civilization?

IJ: Like many Americans, he read *Don Quixote* as a young man. Rolena Adorno has made a compelling case for the influence of a multivolume work called *The World Displayed,* where Irving learned the stories of Boabdil, Columbus, and the Spanish conquest of Mexico and Peru. But it was pure chance that the middle-aged Irving found a job as translator of the recently published Columbus documents in Spain, compiled by Martín Fernández de Navarrete in the 1820s. Irving was at the time wandering aimlessly around Europe, fearing the loss of the reputation he had gained with *The Sketch Book*. He sank his teeth into the Columbus story, out of necessity, one should say, but became the most influential and successful of the early Hispanists.

IS: Irving's biography of Christopher Columbus always struck me as hitting a false note.

IJ: I agree. He wanted to make a hero out of Columbus, a role model that Americans could emulate: the daring, enterprising, visionary man who discovers the New World. By this he meant mostly North America, because what became Spanish America would soon be corrupted by the greed and ambition of the Habsburg monarchs. He aimed well, because his abridged *Columbus* became obligatory reading in the school systems of New York and Massachusetts, the largest at the time in the United States. But there was an edge to Irving's portrayal of the mariner: Columbus was a fanatic, and he brought slavery to the New World. There is also a sarcastic tone in the description of the Spanish companions of Columbus. Some of them look quite ridiculous with their exaggerated views of honor and religious beliefs that border on superstition. They are like obsolete Don Quixotes, caricatures of the real knights who fought during the Reconquista against the Arabs.

IS: How about his views of Arabs?

IJ: He portrays them as superstitious fanatics who cannot control their passions, especially their anger. They know that they are doomed, but they fight with suicidal force nonetheless. I strongly suspect that he had in mind the American Indians, because the tropes used to describe them are quite similar. Some of the Arabs, however, are the stereotypical "Oriental," that is, lovers of luxury and nearly effeminate. This is how he shows them in *Chronicles of the Conquest of Granada* (1829).

IS: I'm thinking of his *Tales of the Alhambra* (1832).

IJ: The Arabs of the *Alhambra* survive only through the now-degraded Spaniards who have retained some of their quaint ways more than three centuries later, when Irving visited the place and fell in love with it. Racial mix must have been a hard subject for Irving to handle, as for many Americans at the time, so that the mix he presents in the *Alhambra* is really a *cultural* mix. The Spaniards of Irving have assumed many of the attributes of the Arabs, especially in storytelling, such as the fascination for hidden treasures and a proneness to "Oriental" laziness.

IS: I'm reminded of a delightful activity I engaged in last summer. I decided to read during my weeks in the beach house in Cape Cod various French and English translations of *The Arabian Nights*. A while back I had read an essay by Borges on the topic. I did the exercise in comparative fashion. Next to me I had Antoine Galland, the seventeenth-century Orientalist whose version of *Les mille et une nuits* was the first to reach the European reader. I also had two English renditions separated by more than a hundred years: one by Richard Burton (1885–1886), the other by Husain Haddawy (1990). (I didn't have access to those by Edward Lane and John Payne.) It's astonishing to realize to what extent translators have been actively involved in rewriting the Persian book. There are episodes, like that of Sinbad, that were later additions, as well as outright forgeries like "The Story of Aladdin and the Magic Lamp"—surprising inserts, given their status as perhaps the most important tales in the compendium.

Needless to say, *The Arabian Nights* has been the ur-text through which to appreciate Oriental customs. As you know, the unifying structure is the role that Shahrazad in keeping King Shahrayar from killing her, as he has done with his previous wives. There aren't really 1,001 stories—that is just a way to refer to the concept of an almost infinite number in Arabic, like our own expression "Lo llamé veinte veces" (I phoned him twenty times). I was flabbergasted by the role sex plays in the narrative. In the Haddawy version, the prologue is called "The Story of King Shahrayar and Shahrazad, His Vizier's Daughter." Two brothers who are kings discover that, while they are away from the palace, their respective wives are sexually promiscuous. The erotic scenes, while not fully explicit, are quite suggestive. At any rate, the kings punish their wives with an atrocious death. This sets the tone for a labyrinthine story by Shahrazad, the vizier's daughter, who, knowing the fate that awaits any woman after a night of sex in King Shahrayar's chambers, asks her father to allow her to spend time with the menacing monarch because, aware of her story-telling talents, she wants to help other women. It is Shahrazad's sister, Dinarzad, who, at the request of Shahrazad, every night asks her sister and, indirectly, the king: "Please, sister, if you are not sleepy, tell us one of your lovely little tales to while away the night." And Shahrazad replies: "With the greatest pleasure."

Each English translator has infused the original with his own agenda. Burton's rendition is outright Victorian. He has a penchant for the gothic style. He likes freaks as well as perverted sexuality. His version of *The Arabian Nights* is biased to the extreme. Haddawy, on the other hand, foolishly believes that a translator is capable of a large degree of objectivity. He approaches the narrative with gloves, as if he were a lab scientist.

In any event, that "Oriental" laziness, for instance, isn't in the book, at least not as laziness is generally understood: a resistance to work, a slowness in movement, a disposition for idleness. In the universe depicted in *The Arabian Nights,* women are indeed lesser creatures than men. Allah is constantly praised, yet numerous demons abound. These demons usually hold a grudge against a master. People believe in magic. And gullibility is a feature in human behavior. More important even is that everything is part of a story that is, in and of itself, organized as a cautionary tale. And stories live within stories. In other words, the world is built as Russian dolls: as one opens up, another one is closed. All in all, a context—joyful, incredulous, and animistic—that is quite different from ours. These features are in sharp contrast with the rigorous rules that define Western civilization, which explains why Western readers usually find these tales to be better suited for children, although that isn't the case.

IJ: A case of misreading . . .

IS: Was Irving's *Alhambra* book successful?

IJ: Enormously, in terms of sales. But it also crystallized the view of Spaniards as "Oriental" and now harmless: the bouts of fanaticism and despotism that brought them to the point of collapse as an empire had now disappeared and turned into distant memories.

IS: What was the reaction to Washington Irving in the Spanish-speaking world? Did his books circulate in Spain?

IJ: They took Spain by storm. There were multiple translations, especially of the *Columbus, Conquest of Granada,* and *Alhambra* books. His ridiculing of Catholicism and the Spanish character was so clever and subtle that most readers missed it. He was even taken seriously by Modesto Lafuente, who cited him often in his groundbreaking history of Spain (*Historia general de España, 1850–1867*), in many ways a model of scholarship. Some of the translations made their way to Spanish America, although for obvious reasons—his subject was really Spain—he was more popular in the peninsula. He was even made a corresponding member of the Royal Academy of History in 1828. His reputation suffered a bit when in the 1840s a Baltimore lawyer by the name of Severn Wallis criticized Irving for giving scant recognition to the considerable work of Spanish historians. But this was not sufficient to stop the demand for his books, some of which are still in print in Spain today.

IS: You also mentioned William Hickling Prescott. I remember experiencing awe when reading, for the first time, his *History of the Conquest of Mexico* (1843). From someone without the research grants that historians are able to secure these days, the scope is impressive. And the narrative power is tremendous. I'm often saddened by the dry and unengaged writing style of contemporary historians. Prescott has the drive of a novelist . . .

IJ: But what an example of the American ambivalence toward the Hispanic world! The mockery of Spanish chivalry, the contempt for despotic and centralized government, the scathing commentary on religious intolerance and inquisitorial obsessions! It's all there in his work, though cleverly disguised as educated and scholarly commentary. I am thinking about his works from *Ferdinand and Isabella* (1837) through the volumes on the conquest of Mexico and Peru. And yet, in the late 1840s, soon after the withdrawal of U.S. troops from Mexico, he begins to undergo an incredible transformation. His playful view of the Hispanic world turns somber, somewhat more sympathetic of the enormous challenges facing Spain as it begins to decline. By the 1850s he himself was declining (he died in 1859), and his sight had deteriorated to the point of near blindness. It seems as if he now wished to correct his early condescending views but couldn't quite manage it. Some of the most macabre scenes and views about the Spanish monarchy are contained in his volumes on Charles V and Philip II, which he left unfinished. One can tell, however, that he is no longer just demonizing Spain but also beginning to understand the magnitude of historical developments.

IS: So he did change his views over time.

IJ: Yes, and there's another important transition in Prescott, a slow but important one from romanticism to objectivity in his approach to history, that becomes dominant toward the end of his life: the respect for evidence. He worked with primary documents and let the evidence take him where it would. It is interesting to see how he led this transition in the historical field. There were others who were doing similar work, like Francis Parkman, John Motley, George Bancroft, and Jared Sparks. But none was as popular and as widely read as Prescott. It is often overlooked that the professionalization of American history really began with Prescott's work on the Hispanic world.

IS: Prescott's blindness has struck me as metaphoric. A handful of writers (Homer, Milton, Borges) were also blind. But they saw beyond their blindness.

IJ: Prescott certainly did. He was not entirely blind, but for the purposes of work he needed to have documents and other narratives read to him. One can imagine him listening and picturing entire situations and events before committing them to print. He also saw through the eyes of others, such as his Scottish friend Fanny Calderón, who was in Mexico when he was writing his *Conquest of Mexico*. She would describe for him the climate, the scenery, the shades of color, and even the aromas of the flora. Much of this made it into Prescott's narrative. At the Massachusetts Historical Society, I found a letter by Caleb Cushing, who was stationed at San Ángel, near Coyoacán, during the Mexican-American War and who told Prescott that he was "struck with the general accuracy of your local descriptions of the face of the country." Clearly, Prescott, perhaps because of his near blindness, worked really hard to inform himself and picture in his mind the situations he described.

IS: In what ways did this group contribute to the foundation of scholarship on Hispanic civilization in the United States?

IJ: The early Hispanists provided the foundations for a growing interest in Hispanic civilization, an interest that the next generation brought to a variety of fields beyond romantic history. The nineteenth-century obsession with archaeology sent many to investigate Maya, Inca, and Aztec ruins. But we miss an approach that addresses the reality of the emerging nations of Latin America. Scholars were interested in practical issues, such as borders. But little by little scholarship expanded, adding new methodologies and yet still keeping some of the early contempt for the Hispanic world. The foundation of many universities in the last quarter of the nineteenth century also meant that there was more systematic research and teaching on the Hispanic world. Helen Delpar's book *Looking South* (2008) does a nice job of describing this evolution.

IS: I like the way you've established the shift between generations, from archaeology to sociopolitics. Either way, there's a condescending approach from U.S. Hispanists to the Hispanic world.

IJ: They probably didn't see it that way, and there were few informed people able to confront them. One notable exception was Severn Wallis, the southerner who challenged Washington Irving for ridiculing his Spanish subjects. Aren't you also condescending in your views of the Hispanic world, Ilan?

IS: It's impossible to escape this dilemma, even when we try hardest. When was Prescott's *History of the Conquest of Mexico* translated into Spanish for the first time?

IJ: The first translation was done by José María de la Vega in 1844, but the true inspiration behind the Mexican edition was Lucas Alamán, who did the annotations to the book and who disagreed with Prescott mostly on religious grounds. The second translation, by Joaquín Navarro, came out in three volumes between 1844 and 1846, just before the war. It was a monumental effort that involved, besides Navarro, Ignacio Cumplido as coordinator of the edition and Isidro Gondra, who was at the time director of the National Museum. Gondra selected and commented on the illustrations. The historian and statesman José Fernando Ramírez provided 124 pages of notes, mostly critical of Prescott's view of the Aztecs.

IS: How about his book on the conquest of Peru?

IJ: The first translation of *History of the Conquest of Peru* (1847) came out in Spain in two volumes between 1847 and 1848, with no indication of translator (Rolena Adorno believes it was Nemesio Fernández Cuesta). We do know about the second translation, by Joaquín García Icazbalceta, which came out in Mexico soon after the war, in 1849. García and Prescott maintained a fluid correspondence for many years, until the historian's death in 1859.

IS: Talk to me more about Fanny Calderón de la Barca and her book *Life in Mexico during a Residence of Two Years in That Country* (1843).

IJ: Fanny (Frances Erskine Inglis) Calderón was a keen-eyed observer and a magnificent writer in the epistolary genre. She was in Mexico for a couple of years in the early 1840s, accompanying her husband, Ángel Calderón, who was the first Spanish ambassador to Mexico after independence. Her *Life in Mexico,* which came out with a preface by Prescott, still stands as a model travel book, but you soon realize that she shared all the prejudices of *la leyenda negra* regarding the Hispanic world.

IS: A fairly uneven view of the Hispanic world. How did all these versions and perversions translate into politics? I'm thinking, for instance, of the filibuster William Walker, who appointed himself president of Nicaragua in 1856.

IJ: Thank you, Ilan. Your comment is a reminder that we've been talking about highly educated people and their complex writings. But clearly there was a lot more, and Walker is a good example. Private individuals realized that in a context of American expansionism they could engage in conquests of their own, and they saw Latin America as fertile ground, often in collaboration with locals. But in the case of filibusters like Walker their politics were tied to the sectional issue in the United States. One of their principal interests was the expansion of slavery. That is one the first things Walker did: to seek the annexation of Nicaragua as a slave state. The unfortunate truth for the political history of Central America is that liberals aided him, and thereby liberalism became synonymous with lawlessness and treachery, unleashing a conservative reaction all over the region.

IS: Ah, the pitfalls of Latin American liberalism: always dreaming of moving forward when, in fact, it commands its stature by being retrograde. It reminds me of that book, *Manual del perfecto idiota latinoamericano* (1996), by Plinio Apuleyo Mendoza, Carlos Alberto Montaner, and Álvaro Vargas Llosa, which poked fun at the follies of the region's "most progressive" movements. The central argument was that, facing clear and present hurdles, the Latin American Left refuses to be practical. And not much has changed since then, I'm afraid. From Hugo Chávez to Evo Morales, the attitude of those in power is often nearsighted.

IJ: Let me change the topic a bit. Your book *The Hispanic Condition* was published in 1995. It depicts Latinos as torn between the here and the there, conflicted about belonging, caught between the past and an unforeseeable future. Have your views changed since then? To what extent were these views a reflection of your own experience coming to the United States?

IS: My views haven't changed much. These were surely the reflections of an immigrant. One of my favorite books at the time was Octavio Paz's *The Labyrinth of Solitude*.

IJ: Which is quite paternalistic toward Chicanos.

IS: Yes. Paz looked at pachucos—as second-generation Mexican Americans from El Paso to Los Angeles were called in the forties— as unworthy. That is, he depreciates any manifestation of Mexican culture in the United States.

IJ: Do you truly believe that Latinos are in eternal conflict?

IS: Yes, I do, although I recognize this to be an intellectual mirage.

IJ: How so?

IS: Intellectuals always need a map to understand the world. But the map isn't the world itself; it's just a replica.

IJ: Have you considered the political implications of some of your views? Your celebration of pluralism and diversity has certainly endeared you to liberal and leftist circles. And yet your rejection of a political identity for Latinos, as victims of dominant groups, is not precisely a radical banner. Likewise, your embrace of the work of Richard Rodriguez, whom you clearly admire, would be anathema to the Left.

IS: I prefer not to be typecast politically. As categories of thought, Right and Left don't do much other than become handcuffs.

IJ: But do you sympathize with the Left?

IS: No, the Left in the Hispanic world is dogmatic. In fact, I often find it idiotic.

IJ: I doubt that the Left has the monopoly on misunderstanding the Hispanic world. Your earlier mention of the case of Samuel Huntington illustrates how the opposite views are just as bad.

IS: The view of the Americas in the United States is marked by condescension.

IJ: How sorry I am to say that this has been, and continues to be, the case. Exceptions notwithstanding, the view of Latin America continues to be that of the nineteenth century. Then, it was race, Catholicism, and engrained despotism that were the subjects that summoned a negative view of the region. Now it is drugs, corruption, and a weakness for populist regimes. Even academics who should know better have trouble understanding that our political history is as rich as that of any country in the world and that our intellectuals have much to contribute to political thought. No. Despite some notable exceptions, we continue to be stuck in carnival, magical realism, and charisma devoid of substance.

IS: The hardest thing for academics is to think for themselves.

IJ: Can things ever change? Serious research can make a difference. But how many people read serious research?

IS: Maybe what we're saying, Iván, is that stereotypes are unavoidable.

IJ: You do, however, expose them. In *The Norton Anthology of Latino Literature,* there are substantial sections on the colonial period as well as on the nineteenth and early twentieth centuries, called, respectively, "Annexation" and "Acculturation."

IS: The anthology includes sections on figures like Spanish explorer Álvar Núñez Cabeza de Vaca and missionaries such as Father Junípero Serra.

IJ: I ask because you have a section that includes three women—Adelina "Nina" Otero Warren, Fabiola Cabeza de Baca Gilbert, and Cleofas Jaramillo—that jointly are described as promoting a Spanish fantasy vision of the Southwest. I'm intrigued by the category . . .

IS: At a time after the Treaty of Guadalupe Hidalgo of 1848, when the United States was already the dominant power in the region, the three looked at the Spanish colonial culture of places like Santa Fe with nostalgia. In their writing they celebrated the past as idyllic.

IJ: Isn't this another version of the same endeavor on which Irving, Prescott, and others embarked? That is, rendering the distant Hispanic past as quaint and bucolic?

IS: Yes, bucolic, meaning false. Their vision was defined by class. They refused to recognize the arrival of a new underclass: the mestizo proletariat.

IVÁN JAKSIĆ: In our second conversation, "*Casticismo* and Empire," you talked about the response by the *modernistas,* from Darío to Martí to the Spanish-American War. And at the end of our previous conversation, "Spreading the Yankee Gospel," you talked about the arrival of the mestizo proletariat at the beginning of the twentieth century. In this chapter, let us discuss the uses of the indigenous past as an ideological weapon.

ILAN STAVANS: With the arrival of independence in the first half of the nineteenth century, emerging nations like Mexico needed to define their collective identity. The *pasado indígena,* the indigenous past, repressed during the colonial period, was again up for grabs. Many newly formed governments did not embrace it indiscriminately. Instead, they endorsed *mestizaje,* the mixed racial background, as their ticket to modernity. The profile of the Indian, which had been interpreted by the missionaries as primitive, idol-worshiping, and socially awkward, retained its undesirable facets. In fact, it was during the *era independiente* when, in more emphatic terms than before, *el indio* became an even more unwelcome type.

IJ: What role does the Latin American intelligentsia play in the shaping of that identity?

IS: A perverse one.

IJ: How so?

IS: To the extent that a collective identity is articulated as a series of intellectual categories, this is a by-product of a middle-class, reflective, self-promoting sensibility. It is manufactured by what Antonio Gramsci called "the organic thinker." That it comes from the middle class is crucial, for it is this class that is always squeezed in between the interests of the haves and the have-nots. The middle class is capable of seeing itself as an abstraction, outside the game, *sub specie aeternitatis.* And that, precisely, is what intellectuals do: they look at society as if from afar. Think of Octavio Paz's concept of the Mexican existing in a maze of solitude.

IJ: A wonderful metaphor . . .

IS: And what is the definition of a metaphor? A simile, a rhetorical trope, a linguistic strategy that uses an image to describe another. I don't believe for a second that Mexicans—and I'm one of them— live in a labyrinth, that we're lonesome people, estranged from our environment, always looking at the precipice of existence. No, Mexicans live just like everyone else: at home, in families at times stable and at others unbalanced, going about their business in life—for example, looking for happiness.

IJ: But do you think that peoples from different backgrounds have distinct cultural characteristics?

IS: No doubt. Yet those traits become philosophical categories only when intellectuals put their brushes on the palette. Let me put it in other words: the United States and Mexico are distinct nations, each with its own personality. One likes fiestas; the other likes parades. One celebrates the Day of the Dead; the other one, Halloween. One loves tequila; the other one, whisky. Should we infer from these dichotomies that Mexico drinks to forget and the United States drinks to have a good time, as Paz suggests?

IJ: Intellectuals love to diagnose.

IS: They surely do . . .

IJ: Don't you?

IS: I'm guilty by association. Writing is thinking. And thinking is making sense of the world, giving it a certain order. But the order of thoughts isn't the order of things. It's crucial to remain humble, to realize the limitations of our own rational chimeras. For instance, an unavoidable touchstone of la hispanidad is Borges.

IJ: Borges, at first sight, does not appear to be a promoter of la hispanidad.

IS: Sure, but only at first sight. A cosmopolitan by nature who was raised by a bifurcated family with roots in England as well as in independence-era Río de la Plata, he spent his life divided between looking at Europe for inspiration and embracing an autochthonous, nativist view of things Hispanic. His autobiographical story "El Sur" is a prime example. The protagonist, Juan Dahlmann, also divided (he's half German, half Argentine), has an accident not unlike the one Borges himself suffered around Christmas 1938, which sent him to the hospital with septicemia. After Dahlmann undergoes surgery—or maybe while the operation is taking place, for the story is a kind of life-after-death description—he finds himself in a bar in a southern neighborhood, about to fight with a bunch of rowdy gauchos. The implication is that Dahlmann is meeting his fate not in the hygienic surgical bed but among his peers.

IJ: Does this tell you something about the weight of the local in Borges's work?

IS: I'm thinking of Borges's disquisition on the difference between gaucho and *gauchesco* literature. Among other places, he developed the topic in an important essay included in *Discusión* (1932) and, later on, in a two-volume anthology he coedited for Fondo de Cultura Económica in Mexico called *La literatura gauchesca.* In the essay, he explains the difference between the literary endeavors produced by the gauchos themselves—by definition, these were just a handful, given that the gauchos didn't come from an educated background—and those produced by urban intellectuals who through their art appropriated the gaucho mythology. Clearly, there's a disquisition on authenticity in what Borges is attempting to explain: gaucho literature, he suggested, might be authentic, but it isn't necessarily rich; in turn, its *gauchesco* counterpart is inauthentic yet plentiful.

IJ: How about Neruda?

IS: I can't think of a more important antennae of la hispanidad. He's your compatriot . . .

IJ: Yes, I read his poems, attended his recitals, and even had a chance to meet him once in the city of Puente Alto when I was a high school student there. But being Chilean does not necessarily give me an authoritative voice to speak about his work. You, on other hand, have devoted a lot of thought and some essential pages of your work to him. Tell me what you see as the fundamental components of his artistic chronology.

IS: After his initiation into poetry with a couple of romantic volumes, most famously *Twenty Love Poems and a Song of Despair* (1923–1924), Neruda moved, as an artist, onto a larger stage. In the various installments of *Residence on Earth,* he explored his native Chile and, afterwards, the Spanish Civil War, where he met, among others, César Vallejo and Octavio Paz.

IJ: What is impressive about Neruda is the scope of his poetry, as was the case with Bello in the nineteenth century.

IS: Neruda, in *Canto general,* attempted a Whitman-like (I was about to write *Whitmanesque* but realized that's a caricature) enterprise of unending ambition. His objective, as you know, was to chronicle the past, present, and future of just about everything in the Americas, from the prehistoric moments to the hopeful tomorrow when a more balanced, less unfair society will be achieved. Thus, *Canto general* is an anthem to what makes us *latinoamericanos.*

IJ: Chile and Neruda are now inextricably connected. There was a time when he was seen as narrowly related to the culture of the political Left. But in post-Pinochet Chile he is a national icon. Chilean National Television recently ran a participatory program to select the ten "greatest" Chileans in history, and Neruda was naturally among them. He was not chosen as *the* greatest, but it is clear that he is now part of the national pantheon. I regret to say that few Chileans are able to recite any of his poems whole, but everyone knows about him. To me, a most important part of his legacy (like that of Gabriela Mistral and Nicanor Parra) is that while riding on the Santiago subway, you can read poetry posted on the interior panels, more often than you see advertisements for exotic vacations or great dishwashers.

IS: The Whitman of Latin America. Pedro Henríquez Ureña once said of Neruda, whom he recognized early on (Henríquez Ureña died in 1946), that the poet made the Spanish language feel new again.

IJ: I know you admire Henríquez Ureña.

IS: Yes, more than a century after his birth (he was born in Santo Domingo, the Dominican Republic, in 1901), Henríquez Ureña offers a model of the Latin American intellectual that remains refreshing. Over the years, I've kept next to me his Charles Eliot Norton Lectures at Harvard for 1940–1941: *The Literary Currents of Hispanic America.* I would love to offer an elaboration of sorts in the same forum one day.

IJ: How so?

IS: Henríquez Ureña looked at Hispanic American literature as a continuum across geographical lines. But the emergence of Latino writing in the United States has forced us to remap the tradition not only beyond those lines but also in linguistic, political, and cultural terms. Nowadays, Cuban, Mexican, and Dominican novelists like Oscar Hijuelos, Sandra Cisneros, and Junot Díaz live in New York City, San Antonio, and Cambridge, Massachusetts, and need to be translated into Spanish.

IJ: And Vallejo?

IS: César Vallejo was far less histrionic than Neruda. His poems on the Spanish Civil War, known as a cycle under the title *España, aparta de mí este cáliz* (*Spain, Take This Chalice from Me*) and left unpublished, are his most accessible. But they are, if I may say so, the least Peruvian, the least Latin American. Of course, everything Vallejo did was a by-product of his Peruvian education. Still, his life in Paris and then Madrid during the Guerra Civil shaped his views dramatically.

IJ: It seems to me that Latin American intellectuals have all, in one way or another, negotiated a difficult compromise between local and universal themes. And sometimes they see the local in totally abstract or idiosyncratic ways.

IS: There is Octavio Paz's view of the Mexican as trapped in a labyrinth. My critique of him appears in my book *Octavio Paz: A Meditation* (2001). His views of the *peladito,* as Mexico's street-smart is known, and the pachuco in Mexican culture—do they truly belong to the nation's psyche, or are they the ruminations of a middle-class intellectual obsessed with describing culture as a Lévi-Strauss type?

IJ: Couldn't it be that he and others are addressing an ideal audience, elsewhere, that likes those sorts of generalizations? V. S. Naipaul, in his *The Return of Eva Perón,* talks about local intellectuals who seek approval and readership abroad. Certainly, the Latin American literary boom of the sixties and seventies created a huge readership for intellectuals.

IS: Not long ago, I wrote a piece for the *Los Angeles Times* about Fidel Castro's question-and-answer (with Ignacio Ramonet) cum autobiography. It was an embarrassing book, allowing El Líder a free ride.

IJ: What do you mean?

IS: No serious questions were asked by Ramonet. Regardless, the Cuban Revolution inaugurated yet another approach to la hispanidad.

IJ: Like all revolutions, it did at first revive the hopes of many intellectuals for social justice. But many of them became quickly disillusioned. The writings inspired in the Cuban Revolution did not in the end contribute much to understanding la hispanidad beyond a highly ideological and distorted view of Latin American society and history. Think, for instance, about Eduardo Galeano's *Open Veins of Latin America* (1971), with which Hugo Chávez is hoping to enlighten President Barack Obama about the predicament of the region. I. F. Stone, the radical U.S. journalist, once said that "every government is run by liars."

IS: Carlos Fuentes, in *The Buried Mirror,* offers a portrait of Hispanic civilization as an ongoing search for identity.

IJ: That might or might not be the case, but it is certainly a more sophisticated and better informed essay than Galeano's. I'm somewhat optimistic about the new generation of intellectuals who are concerned about the region as a whole, as well as their individual nations. An ambitious effort like Jorge Volpi's *El insomnio de Bolívar* (*Bolívar's Insomnia,* 2009) is light years ahead of Galeano and many others in between. And in comparison with Paz's attempt, there is much more sophistication concerning Latinos in the United States. You have followed this history more closely.

IS: Chicanismo, an aesthetic that developed around the Chicano movement in the late sixties, is often ignored in Latin American intellectual circles. However, its value is uncontestable. It was an aesthetic of the downtrodden, the abused, and the colonized that was eager to subvert the status quo. It came about in the sixties, in the midst of the civil rights era in the United States.

IJ: You've said that to this day the civil rights era is presented—in the media, political circles, and educational texts—as a black-versus-white confrontation.

IS: It was something far larger: the seed for the multicultural change about to take place in the country a mere decade later. Along with blacks, Latinos (e.g., Mexicans and Puerto Ricans) and Filipinos played an important role. Not too long ago, I reviewed for the *San Francisco Chronicle* an anthology of political speeches, published under the aegis of the Library of America. I was astonished not to find a single entry by a Chicano, not even one.

IJ: Publishers, like libraries and bookstores, have a way of classifying or lumping together materials that should be integrated. Yet you've edited Cesar Chavez's speeches in *An Organizer's Tale* (2008) and released a photographic essay of his quest to improve the conditions of farmworkers in the Southwest (2010).

IS: The projects were largely in response to the lack of representation I find on the standard American bookshelf, which tends to ghettoize people by class, skin color, and language. However, I sometimes feel it is a lost battle. In truth, I sought to achieve something else too. A necessary icon, Chavez has been placed—lazily, no doubt—on a pedestal as *the* Latino activist par excellence. Nothing he did seems faulty. But the truth is dramatically different. Journalist Miriam Pawel wrote an investigative reportage that was serialized in the *Los Angeles Times* and served as the basis for her book *The Union of Their Dreams* (2009). It follows the life of eight people intimately connected with Chavez and the United Farm Workers, explaining the corrupt environment that developed at the union and the intense power struggles that in the end brought it down. I eagerly awaited the publication of Pawel's book. She portrays Chavez as a warmhearted visionary who in the last third of his career was poorly advised on the political, economic, and labor fronts. Are we able to understand Chavez with more nuance, thanks to her? I'm not sure. Reviews appeared in major publications on the West Coast but not on the East Coast, perhaps because the Chicano movement—and, might I say, the civil rights era as well?—is seen nationally through a bipolar lens, as an affair largely fought in the West and the South, although the envoys were from the East. Whatever the case might be, union cofounder Dolores Huerta, on Univision, denounced the portrait as a pack of lies. Initially, the Cesar E. Chavez Foundation, in charge of keeping the leader's memory alive, attacked Pawel in its blog but then opted to keep its mouth shut in order to expand the debate.

IJ: Was Chavez an inspiring orator?

IS: He had only an elementary education. He was a self-educated man who, at the invitation of community organizers like Saul Alinsky and Fred Ross, started reading the works of Henry Thoreau, Mahatma Gandhi, and, later on, the Reverend Martin Luther King Jr. His ideas on nonviolence emerged from the personal readings he did on his own and from his Christian faith. When compared to more polished speakers, Chavez was rather flat, repetitive, and unstructured. His speeches never developed an argument; they simply reiterated a series of truisms. Still, it is important to remember where he came from and, perhaps more importantly, whom he spoke to. He was a leader capable of using his rhetoric to bring down an empire, as Gandhi did. For the most part, Chavez communicated with illiterate, impoverished migrant workers. He knew the way to their heart because he spoke in their language. Neither in a higher, lofty note, nor in a condescending fashion. He used plain street talk, unpolished, unadulterated.

IJ: How does Chicanismo revise the concept of la hispanidad?

IS: A fascinating question. Chicanismo is the ideology behind, or maybe derived from, the Chicano movement of the late sixties and seventies, in which Mexican Americans fought for better labor conditions and for civil rights in the context of a larger social struggle with similar objectives that was sweeping the United States. This ideology perceived itself to be at a juncture: it was rooted in the struggle for self-determination of Indians in Mexico and for social justice, freedom, and autonomy as represented in the fight by Cubans under the then-inspiring revolution led by Fidel Castro and his Argentine friend Ernesto "Che" Guevara. But Chicanos didn't see themselves as Mexicans. They had a troubled relationship with Mexico, the country from which some, though not all of, their ancestors had come. I say "not all" because a portion of the Chicano population, especially in Arizona, Colorado, New Mexico, and Utah, traced its roots to the aboriginal population during the colonial period and, even further, to the mythical homeland of Aztlán.

IJ: A sort of Shangri-La.

IS: Indeed, a foundational place from which Chicanos trace their origins. The legend suggests that the Aztecs, a nomadic tribe, migrated to what was Tenochtitlán, known today as Ciudad de México, left a place somewhere in the state of Nayarit, or maybe even north of the Rio Grande, that was known as Aztlán. This means they are older than Mexicans. This means also that Chicanos did not descend from Mexicans but vice versa. In any case, the Chicanos of the sixties weren't looking for support from Mexico. The most radical fought for self-determination. They wanted to revise the outcome of the Treaty of Guadalupe Hidalgo, signed in 1848, after the Mexican-American War, in which two-thirds of Mexico's territory was sold to the United States for $15 million. I say "revise" and not "reverse": their mission was to free themselves from American occupation, to be autonomous, to be independent.

IJ: Was that the objective of Cesar Chavez and other leaders as well?

IS: Not quite. Chavez was a labor organizer. His political views were more immediate. He didn't dream of Shangri-La. What he wanted was to better the conditions of Mexican migrant laborers in the Southwest. Other Chicano leaders like Dolores Huerta, Reies López Tijerina, Rodolfo "Corky" Gonzales, and even a loose cannon like the lawyer Oscar "Zeta" Acosta, a.k.a. the Brown Buffalo, fought for social justice. On occasion Acosta might have talked of secession, but given that he was a drug addict constantly running away from the law, his political speeches were seen as psychedelic reveries.

IJ: Over the years, you have developed a strong interest in Chicanismo.

IS: I find Chicano history and identity enormously compelling. I'm a Mexican Jew with no direct connection to Chicanos other than my intellectual pursuits.

IJ: In fact, you're quite controversial among militant Chicanos.

IS: They see me as an interloper.

IJ: Why?

IS: Because any alien poring over their affairs is automatically described as an intruder. There's a certain allergy to free inquiry and enterprise in the community. But it's okay by me: the role of the intellectual is not to please people but to make all of us think. What's your connection, if any, with Chicanos? Maybe through your students or through your family?

IJ: In New York State, at least during my student days in the seventies, the predominant Hispanic population was Puerto Rican. I moved to California in 1982, a state with a very strong Chicano presence and Chicano studies programs in several universities, including Berkeley, where I first went as a postdoctoral researcher. In between, love intervened, because I met my wife of twenty-seven years in Buffalo, and we both moved to California after our marriage. She is Mexican American from Kansas City, so I had the wonderful experience, in the United States, to relive what was familiar to me: an immigrant family with many locally born children. We could switch from Spanish to English and relate in all the ways that define the Latino experience in the United States. But there was something else: their strongest bond was to Mexico, and that sense of the *patria,* even though it is not exclusionary, struck me as a vibrant expression of belonging and identity. Some Chicanos do reach out, in genuine ways, to other Latinos, but in my family's case their strong link is to Mexico. In California I met Chicano academics who became dear friends, but they were torn between working on Mexican topics, or on U.S. or state public policy concerning Latinos. Some did both, and really well. But overall they had a more political orientation than did and do members of my family in Missouri. Chicanos are constantly navigating between their sense of origin and their desire to belong and be recognized in the United States. But it goes beyond that, as Chicanos along with other Latinos make claims and do speak as equals in U.S. society. Much creativity and gravitas lie behind what they do. But there are also competing approaches and agendas, as shown by Richard Rodriguez.

IS: Richard Rodriguez is one of the most complex—and evasive—thinkers in the U.S. Latino tradition. Although he is close to the nineteenth-century transcendentalist tradition, it often feels to me as if he were French, so amorphous is his style.

IJ: You describe a conversation with Richard Rodriguez in the last section of your autobiography, *On Borrowed Words* (2001).

IS: Over the years, we have met in whatever place we coincide. He's a terrific friend. I came across his autobiography upon arriving in the United States in 1985 and immediately defined my own self against his public persona.

IJ: Could you describe it?

IS: He is loathed by Chicanos, and, in my opinion, he thrives on being the target of such hatred. The animosity comes from his attack on affirmative action. Of course, he knows the program well, since he himself is a product of it. *Hunger of Memory* details his ambivalence toward the program. All this is precisely what I admire in Rodriguez: his willingness to use his own case to show the pitfalls of being labeled an "ethnic" in a multicultural society. However, I have trouble with his reluctance to take the road of controversy all the way through.

IJ: What do you mean?

IS: Some years ago, he was invited to lecture in one of the state universities in California. The Chicanos on campus organized a series of protests. Rather than engage them, Rodriguez foolishly canceled the stint. By the way, the refusal to accept criticism, I believe, is a feature of a particular generation of Chicano intellectuals. I have several colleagues, all of them veteran literary critics and folklorists, who constantly tell their students not to openly criticize a Chicano writer because by doing so they will join forces with the enemy. It's a terrible attitude!

IJ: Criticism should be perceived as constructive.

IS: And it's an essential feature in a democratic, tolerant society. Without criticism, our view of the world has no depth. ·

IJ: Let's return to a topic you and I have addressed on and off throughout these conversations: the Latin American Left. In particular, I want us to talk about the Venezuelan leader Hugo Chávez.

IS: Chávez plays the Bolívar card. He sees himself as an incarnation of the nineteenth-century dream of unification of Latin America.

IJ: As I suggested earlier, that is little more than a cynical appropriation of Bolívar's statements and actions, mixed with a stale concoction of Marxist categories and the scattered views of Fidel Castro. At the level of conceptual consistency, there is nothing. But as an ideology that resonates with vulnerable segments of the population, and some neo-Marxist intellectuals, it works.

IS: Yet those empty ideas often steer the masses.

IJ: But for how long? I doubt that it will go much beyond Chávez himself. By the way, I admire the penetrating analyses of scholars like Germán Carrera Damas, John Lynch, and David Bushnell, who were clear about all this from the start, and I have said so. Scholarship can truly help put these issues in context.

IS: Yet scholarship is reactive, not active. Do you agree? The urgency of a demagogue like Hugo Chávez makes research look painfully passive. What interests me, however, is how an idea from the past suddenly acquires currency. Why do you think Bolívar still matters?

IJ: Regarding Bolívar's durability as an icon, he will always matter as a historical figure. He is simply inescapable. Everywhere you look in Spanish America, you will find a street, a monument, a town, or a major landmark that bears his name. Academics, myself included, continue to work on his political ideas, the context in which he lived and died, and his legacy. The reality is that he liberated much of what is today Spanish America. But what you are saying, Ilan, is that periodically some politician, party, or movement will appropriate some aspect of Bolívar's thought, spin it, and sell it as a new mantra for solving the problems of the region. The Left, though I should say the old Marxist and populist Left, has been winning this ideological battle, but it is not rare to find conservatives upholding some of his ideas, especially regarding order and stability, or his statements about the lack of political virtues among Spanish Americans. Again, Bolívar was not a systematic thinker, and so there is much room to use bits and pieces of his speeches or writings for whatever purpose. Also, since he himself identified with Don Quixote, it is pertinent to reflect on how icons acquire a life of their own. How many who talk familiarly about Don Quixote have actually read the book? How many who invoke Bolívar actually know him? I dare say that Hugo Chávez himself would not pass a test. But I recognize your main point: intellectuals thus far have been unable to counter the new Bolivarian barrage.

IS: A barrage, indeed. In my eyes, Chávez is a buffoon.

IJ: And yet he does represent something, or at least capitalizes on people's need for some form of political identity to overcome exclusion. Wouldn't this be the case of *indigenismo*?

IS: The questions raised by *indigenismo* will never die. It was a feature of the late nineteenth and twentieth centuries, and it continues to agitate. This is because its ferment is what Latin America is made of.

IJ: *Indigenismo* might be an important issue in the twenty-first century, but it is not without antecedents, going as far back as Bartolomé de Las Casas and the many chroniclers who carefully recorded indigenous traditions in order to rescue their past or defend Indians against predatory conquistadors. In the late eighteenth and early nineteenth centuries, there was also a glorification of the Indian past that provided an important basis for the movements for independence. There were plenty of intellectuals, especially in Mexico, who thought long and hard about the place of Indians and mestizos in the new republic. Elsewhere, writers like Jorge Isaacs and Clorinda Matto de Turner called attention to the plight of their indigenous compatriots. But *indigenismo,* as we know it today, is a product of the great revolutions and movements of the twentieth century. Think about the Mexican Revolution and its heavily *indigenista* orientation up through the regime of Lázaro Cárdenas. Or think about José Vasconcelos's *Indología* (1927), which argued compellingly in favor of incorporating Indians into national life. Most such schemes, however, were inclusive, in that they did not mean a return to indigenous traditions but rather their acknowledgment and celebration. Visually, one cannot but think of the murals of Diego Rivera and José Clemente Orozco, in which Indians become fused in a larger tradition of struggle against oppressions of all sorts. So *indigenismo* gets to be a part of la hispanidad rather than the other way around. When the Peruvian APRA (Alianza Popular Revolucionaria Americana) proposed that the region be called Indoamérica, its leaders were not thinking about returning to Inca ways of life or entirely changing Western patterns of economic development. And when José Carlos Mariátegui wrote approvingly of the Inca Empire, he was mostly interested in how socialist (in a modern sense) it appeared to be. But all in all, *indigenismo* really brought awareness that indigenous peoples were part of our national mosaic and that there was much to celebrate in their traditions and contributions. The most recent incarnations of *indigenismo,* however, are more highly politicized and have invited secession, as in the case of Chiapas in Mexico in the early 1990s, or fragmentation, as is going on as of this writing in 2010 in Evo Morales's Bolivia. One also needs to consider the role of humanitarian and environmental international organizations in fomenting a form of ethnic struggle against the national state wherever economic development projects are launched.

IS: Some years ago I worked on a translation into English, done by John Polt, of Vasconcelos's *The Cosmic Race* (1925).

IJ: It's important to place Vasconcelos in the context of positivism, for he was clearly reacting against this dominant school during the Porfiriato, as the years of Porfirio Díaz's rule are known. Like many other anti-positivists around the region, he countered the alleged materialism of the positivists with a spiritual version of what characterized Latin America and its people. In many ways, he was engaged in the same endeavor as José Enrique Rodó, but his emphasis was more on the positive aspects of *la raza cósmica,* especially its indigenous components. He was a great agitator but a terrible politician; he abandoned his own supporters when he lost in the presidential elections of 1929 and later dallied with fascism.

IS: Political activism is a sine qua non of Latin American identity.

IJ: Things might be changing today, when a growing segment of the population finds satisfaction of their needs in the market economy rather than in politics. But for our own generation, and countless others before us, politics was a central part of life.

IS: My own political awakening came in the eighties, while I was a college student in the most Left-leaning university in Mexico, the Universidad Autónoma Metropolitana. After the student upheaval of 1968, which resulted in the October massacre in Tlatelolco Square, the government decided it was too dangerous to concentrate young people in a couple of academic institutions: the Universidad Nacional Autónoma de México (a.k.a. UNAM) and the Instituto Politécnico Nacional (a.k.a. Poli). President Gustavo Díaz Ordaz and his powerful cabinet member Luis Echeverría Álvarez, later also a president himself, pushed for a decentralized student body by establishing a new university that would be divided into three branches, spread throughout the nation's capital. I was enrolled in the most militant of the three, the one in Xochimilco. (The other two were Azcapotzalco and Ixtapalapa.) The place at the time was a *semillero de activistas,* an activists' nursery. Argentine exiles, running away from their country's military dictatorship, had settled in Mexico. A large number of them were teachers, artists, and psychoanalysts. Many of my professors belonged to that group.

It was in those years, between 1980 and 1984, that I traveled to Oaxaca, Yucatán, and Chiapas. I also worked with a theater troupe. And I volunteered with Padre Chinchachoma, a fascinating Catholic priest who spent his energy redeeming (or trying to redeem) *niños callejeros,* orphans living on the street.

IJ: How?

IS: Padre Chinchachoma's view was that the *niños callejeros* were deprived of love—paternal love, sibling love, societal love—but not God's love. His mission was to love these children with all his heart in order to prove that, though abandoned, they weren't forgotten, at least not by him. To achieve his goal, he sacrificed everything: money, comfort, a bourgeois life. He lived with the orphans in abandoned homes, and once he got their trust, he brought them to live in a special home he administered for them.

IJ: A moving story...

IS: While working with Padre Chinchachoma, I came to realize the imbalances that afflicted Mexico. I had been raised in a middle-class home. I knew, in general terms, what the country was like. But only after being exposed to eight-year-olds sniffing gasoline, smoking pot, and getting drunk on cheap beer did I realize the extent of the misery.

IJ: What was your reaction?

IS: Anxiety, frustration, pain. I wanted to help—and I did. I became an activist, attending marches, participating in neighborhood meetings, joining militant groups. The Mexican Communist Party played a prominent role on the Xochimilco campus, and I followed along its path, as did several of my friends. One of them was Fidel Castro's niece. With her I traveled to Cuba. My classmates became prominent photographers, filmmakers, and political consultants.

My experience in Mexico was dramatically different from yours in South America. There were *desaparecidos,* for sure, but the Mexican government used its tentacles in more subtle ways. Since 1929 the country had lived in a one-party dictatorship. The PRI (Partido Revolucionario Institucional) controlled every type of news and information that reached the population. Every six years, whenever there was a presidential election, the winner would be announced on the front pages of major newspapers on the morning the voting booths would open. It was a farce!

IJ: What did you get out of those years?

IS: The realization that, for as much as one fights, progress is a mirage. The biblical prophet Jeremiah said: "The harvest is past, the summer is ended, and we are not saved." Only later, when the neoliberal free market policies entered into play, did I realize how foolish my efforts had been. Deep in my heart I believe in equality, although

I know it can't be achieved. I'm a skeptic, which is probably a result of age. Humans are always building hierarchies. Capitalism and communism are two sides of the same coin. In both of them a small elite is always in power. Your political awakening was different, though.

IJ: Yes, the Chile of my youth had a highly mobilized civil society. Political parties were very much a part of the fabric of national life. People got socialized into them willingly, just as one would join a soccer club. I am talking about normal times, however. In the sixties, real polarization occurred, and Chilean society was brought to the breaking point. Scholars speak of a "hypermobilization" that led to the military coup of 1973, and they are not wide off the mark. But the reality is that the imposition of a brutal dictatorship changed politics as we knew it, perhaps forever. We were now facing not only the suspension of all political activity but also the killing and disappearance of opponents of military rule. If the first had been a normal political awakening, the second had been an entrance into a nightmare from which it was nearly impossible to wake. The legacies of this dictatorial period remain, and they are still like an open wound in the body politic of so many Latin American countries. I lived through the worst part of it in Chile and Argentina and can attest to the reality of the abductions, the torture, and the atrocious killings. But what was absolutely maddening was the denial on the part of the governments, a feeling I share with you as you describe political events in Mexico. In South America the so-called Operación Cóndor shows that the military governments' coordination of killings and disappearances across their borders was deliberate, as was their determination to obfuscate or to shamelessly lie regarding the whereabouts of their victims. In post-Pinochet Chile the Concertación governments (1990–2010) went a long way to identify the crimes and provide redress, but they were not able to secure full military cooperation to find the remains of people killed during the Pinochet regime. Other countries have decided just to shut the door to any further inquiries. But until the fate of the missing is known, and justice delivered, we will not overcome this traumatic period.

IS: In the twentieth century, student activism was an essential component of Hispanic identity. When I was a student at the Universidad Autónoma Metropolitana–Xochimilco, not to complain publicly, not to march, not to agitate was to be a *vendido* (sellout). I'm a professor in an elite liberal arts college in New England. Supposedly students are more passive in my institution—and indeed they are. Still, the attitude of a Latino student when arriving at my office is different from that of other students: Latino students feel their rights have been wronged for generations and deserve to be revisited. I don't doubt this is true, but the way to achieve that revisitation isn't only through activism. Activism is a tool for change. Scholarship, I'm convinced, is another one.

IJ: I want you to develop this thought, Ilan.

IS: I don't believe in passive scholarship.

IJ: What do you mean?

IS: Knowledge is change. To know is to engage the world, to transform it. I respect enormously a scholar like you who spends years delving into a topic in order to understand what it means. The outcome will make people see things differently. But I also support a proactive scholarship in which the researcher gets his hands dirty in the present.

IJ: How so?

IS: Take Spanglish. It's a phenomenon dozens of academics thoroughly dislike because it erases the borders between languages. One approach to it, taken by scores of my colleagues, has been to study Spanglish in isolation, through the tools of sociolinguistics. By "isolation" I mean to appreciate what a Spanglish speaker whose conversations have been recorded does in her verbal transactions: what syntactical devices she uses, and when and why. The outcome is released in refereed journals, which are read by interested peers. That's a laudable effort, and I do it myself constantly. But another approach is to use that outcome to return to society. That is, to talk to the media about what Spanglish is, who its speakers are, et cetera. The purpose is to engage the public in a dialogue, to disseminate knowledge. In my opinion, that's activist scholarship. That opinion, I suspect, might be traced to my student years in Mexico.

IJ: We are a product of our environment.

IS: Were you involved in student politics?

IJ: Yes. I attended a trade school in Puente Alto, a working-class city south of Santiago. The great majority of my classmates were children of either communist or socialist families. This was in the 1960s, so you can imagine the level of political concern that stirred us. It was not purely ideological, though, as high unemployment and inflation made our prospects quite dismal, trained as we were to become machinists (as in my case), electricians, carpenters, and skilled workers in a variety of other crafts. So we wanted opportunities, as well as more access to higher education. I became part of the student government in my school, and in short order I became a regional and then a national delegate for the Chilean organization of trade schools. From a very young age I became aware of parliamentary procedures, crafting of agreements and statements, and the power to call strikes. And when we exercised the latter, they were massive. In one of those strikes the president of my school's student government was arrested, and I became the de facto leader. My first action was to try to get him released, and for that I had to muster all my presence of mind to ride to the capital, Santiago; reach the national senate; and seek the help of the late Volodia Teitelboim, who is now better known as a writer but who was always a stalwart member of the Communist Party. He did help to get our leader released, I should say, to my great relief. We went on with our movements until the election of Salvador Allende in 1970 gave us a temporary respite. By the time of the Unidad Popular government, I was in college and no longer involved in student politics, except that at one stage I participated in a movement to secure housing for homeless workers. But not being active in politics in 1973 did not save me or my friends. The military regime went after us with a vengeance.

IS: The experience must have marked you forever.

IJ: Certainly, but I insist that political involvement was normal in democratic Chile. I believe that student activism is in our national DNA in Chile, and perhaps elsewhere in Latin America. This has been the case historically since early in the twentieth century. Many of our national leaders have emerged out of the student movement, which has traditionally provided the recruitment grounds for the leaders of most major political parties. Today this is different, as students find other ways to achieve their aims in what is now a market-driven society. But the impulse is there. As recently as 2006 the Chilean student movement presented the new government of Michelle Bachelet with a serious challenge. I would not be surprised if some of these high school student leaders will in time become national politicians or leaders.

IS: What is your pedagogical philosophy? What do you expect to achieve in the classroom? And what do you hope to accomplish in your relationship with students?

IJ: Let me first say that I was privileged to have an outstanding mentor in Chile, Juan Rivano, who was not only my philosophy teacher but also my mentor in many other ways. He detected quite early that I was struggling with my vocation. I had studied sociology for a year but did not like it, so I moved to philosophy, but initially without much conviction. I was torn at the time by my love of literature and writing, but I could not see myself as a student of literature. So he wisely encouraged my literary interests while keeping me focused on philosophy. He taught logic, without which philosophy is really undisciplined speculation. He taught me how to appreciate philosophy, with great patience, to the point that I did quite well in the most difficult course he taught, called theory of knowledge, which was really advanced logic. In normal circumstances I would have finished my studies with him and followed in his footsteps in the field. But the military coup intervened. He was taken by the secret police from his house one night during curfew and kept incommunicado until he surfaced in a notorious prison camp called Tres Alamos. He spent a year in another prison camp on the coast, called Puchuncaví. I visited him as often as I was allowed to see him. It was in that horrible situation, for few but intense hours at a time, in makeshift visiting quarters surrounded by armed soldiers, that I could appreciate the philosopher and the human being in him. He was oblivious to his own personal situation. Instead he worried about my now-independent studies and guided my progress with pointed directions. But he also taught me the virtue of patience by example. I swore then, and I hope to keep my promise, that patience and endurance would be the values I would pursue in any area where I could finally find a place for myself. Yes, because our lives were so drastically changed and we all ended up in different places. He was thrown out of the country and moved to Israel first and then to Sweden, where he still lives. My own trek took me to the United States, to American studies and then history. But he left me with an unforgettable and most valuable tool for going through this life.

IS: Which is?

IJ: What I learned from him is what I try to do with my own students: help them find their true calling and then give them the tools to persevere in their choice. But you know how rare this is. When I was in a position to teach in the United States, a college education was no longer a privilege but more and more like an entitlement. Students were also becoming more like sophisticated consumers. Yet here and there I found students who were eager to get more than a mark on their tests. I doubt that I have been able to do for them what my mentor did for me, but I keep trying. Today the students I teach are roughly the age I was when I had to leave the country, so I know what I can expect of them, if they wish to know the range of experiences a person of that age might. This may not be necessarily useful to them, but it is for those who seek a sense of their human potential.

IS: In Mexico I had a theater teacher, Héctor Azar, who once said to me, "You shouldn't give the audience what the audience wants. Instead, you should teach the audience to want something different."

IJ: It's a valuable lesson useful for teachers.

IS: It's a trick lesson too. Héctor Azar was an avant-garde stage director. His goal wasn't to entertain the public but to make the audience curious, eager to be challenged. I agree with you: one can't achieve this with every student. But do you know what the Talmud, the enduring exegetical Jewish book, states, Iván? That to save a single life is to save the world entire. If I'm allowed to paraphrase the sentence, I'd say that to teach a single student in effective fashion is to teach the world entire.

IVÁN JAKSIĆ: As you've suggested countless times, Ilan, there is an intricate connection between Spanish as a language of empire and the concept of la hispanidad. And between how a language is structured and how people process thought.

ILAN STAVANS: Language is not only about word choice but also about a way of articulating identity. Spanish, in its multiple vicissitudes, contains in itself the DNA of Hispanic civilization. But let us begin with our own experience with the Spanish language.

IJ: Spanish was the dominant language in my hometown, but there were other languages spoken. In addition there was a heavy influence of the Spanish spoken by migrants from Chiloé, a large island to the north of Punta Arenas but still some one thousand kilometers from the central valley of Chile. So I was aware of at least some differences in pronunciation and word choice. The shock came when I moved to Santiago, where the Spanish spoken is so different, closer in some respects to the Spanish spoken in southern Spain.

IS: Did you understand?

IJ: I could not understand half of the words, much less the intonation and the colloquialisms. It was truly like learning another language. The formal Spanish was clearly recognizable to me, and that is the Spanish I embraced, though enriched, I think, by the worldview behind the language spoken in Santiago. The people of the central valley are so much more lively, adventurous, and humorous. I was inevitably drawn to that lifestyle, although I retained some of my southern parsimony and reserve. College really opened new language possibilities for me, as I explored the world of philosophy and abstract thinking. I wrote quite a bit, including fiction and poetry. I reached the point of comfort and mastery of the language, at least for my age. But then, at the age of twenty, I had to leave for Argentina, where I worked long days and weekends as a machinist. And then, at twenty-two, I was in the United States, trying to learn an entirely different language. I kept up with my Spanish by reading and by conversing with a now-wider range of Spanish speakers. Inevitably, however, I lost the fluency, especially in writing, that I had achieved prior to the coup. These days I write a lot more in Spanish and talk a lot more of it too. I love the language but wonder what would have happened if I had kept at it nonstop.

IS: I've undergone a similar experience. My departure from Mexico in 1985 and my adoption of English as my primary way of communication today made me rethink my relationship with Spanish.

IJ: That rethinking has been fruitful. You've produced an array of enlightening studies on language in general and on the history of Spanish in particular.

IS: To be away from one's home (I'm looking at Spanish as *el hogar*) is to know its true worth.

IJ: The Spanish newspaper *ABC* once called you "our modern Antonio de Nebrija."

IS: Antonio de Nebrija is an emblematic figure. Through the years and in different projects, I keep on coming back to him. It was Nebrija who published the first *Gramática* of the Spanish language. It came out in 1492, the same year Columbus embarked on his first voyage across the Atlantic and the Jews were expelled from the Iberian Peninsula. In the dedication to Queen Isabella, Nebrija talked of language, and he was making a reference to the Spanish language in particular, as *la compañera del imperio.*

IJ: The companion of empire.

IS: Although Nebrija gets the credit, there is a history prior to him about the vernacular in the Iberian Peninsula. Think of the pressure in intellectual circles to conform to linguistic standards. For instance, in recent years I've pondered why the Jewish and Muslim poets of medieval Spain aren't part of the so-called national canon. In the case of Jews, a crop I know better, the offering is plentiful: Avraham ibn Ezra, Yehuda Alharizi, Avraham ibn Hasdai, Todros Abulafia, Vidal Benveniste . . . La Convivencia might have offered a change for dialogue, but the fact that they are Jewish disqualified them in the post-1492 periods and up to the present. There is another decisive factor too: almost all wrote in Arabic and Hebrew. The building of the nation, as you know, depends on a pledge of alliance to the vernacular, even when that vernacular is still in the making. A curious exception—if that is what indeed it is—is Santob de Carrión (Shem Tov Ardutiel). Born in the late thirteenth century and dead after 1345, he apparently served King Alfonso XI in state affairs, as he was fluent in three languages: Castilian, Arabic, and Hebrew. He is known as the author of *Proverbios morales,* which, as the title suggests, was written in Spanish. The proverbs were an inspiration to Antonio Machado, also from Old Castile, who modeled his own proverbs after de Carrión's. That de Carrión wrote these snippets of wisdom in Spanish makes him a candidate to the Iberian literary canon. His status in it, nevertheless, is problematic in that if and when *Proverbios morales* is read, his Jewishness isn't regularly factored in. By the way, a similar emptying of religious identity took place as Shlomo ibn Gabirol's *Fons vitae (Fountain of Life)* became an influential Neoplatonic source in scholastic philosophy only after it was translated from Arabic, its original language, into Latin. In Arab circles, ibn Gabirol (1021/1022–c. 1057/1058) was known as Abu Ayyub Sulaiman ibn Yahya ibn Jabirul, and during the Renaissance among Latin scholars, as Avicebron. At any rate, in Nebrija's *Gramática* there's an attempt to embrace Spanish as a viable intellectual conduit. Keep in mind that, in his time, Latin was the language of the educated elite, the language of learning.

IJ: A language like Spanish, which developed historically under so many different influences prior to full literacy and the predominance of grammars, must have inevitably reflected the spirit of its people. One might read old medieval Spanish with some difficulty, but the sounds are there, the short sentences are there, the issues that motivate people and touch their hearts are there. Even in Golden Age drama and poetry, the Spanish language is strikingly simple and yet so evocative.

IS: And baroque.

IJ: The beauty of the language is that it has retained its fundamental simplicity and directness over the centuries and that certain sounds and words continue to resonate for us across countries and ages.

IS: Francisco de Quevedo has a memorable sonnet to Don Pedro Girón, Duque de Osuna:

> Faltar pudo su patria al grande Osuna,
> Pero no a su defensa sus hazañas;
> Diéronle muerte y cárcel las Españas,
> De quien él hizo esclava la Fortuna.
>
> Lloraron sus envidias una a una
> Con las propias naciones las extrañas;
> Su tumba son de Flandes las campañas,
> Y su epitafio la sangrienta luna.
>
> En sus exequias encendió el Vesubio
> Parténope, y Trinacria al Mongibelo;
> El llanto militar creció en diluvio.
>
> Diole el mejor lugar Marte en su cielo;
> La Mosa, el Rhin, el Tajo y el Danubio
> Murmuran con dolor su desconsuelo.

It isn't easy to translate Quevedo into English . . .

IJ: You prefer to leave the original imprisoned in its own language.

IS: Yes, every language is a prison. But I do want to focus on the astonishing line concluding the second quartet: "Y su epitafio la sangrienta luna" (And his epitaph the bleeding moon). The moon is the Duque de Osuna's witness; it is also his epitaph. The Duque de Osuna is a surrogate for each and every one of us. The same moon that witnessed his death in Flandes (Flanders) looks at us from above every night. Likewise with language: the same words you and I use—in Spanish, *amor, manzana, Dios*—have resonated in the ears of our ancestors. And they'll be echoed in the ears of our successors.

IJ: Your rendition of the verse is beautiful, but is it faithful? Some scholars see "sangrienta luna" as a reference to the Turkish Empire, against which Osuna fought. Also, wouldn't *sangrante* be a closer translation of "bleeding"? To me, *sangrienta* could translate as "bloody." If you interpret *luna* as a symbol of empire, then the reference to a "bloody empire" makes sense.

IS: That's the approach that James O. Crosby, the U.S. Hispanist who specialized in Quevedo, took. He was right: Pedro Téllez-Girón y Velasco Guzmán y Tovar, Duque de Osuna, who attempted to modernize the Spanish Armada, defeated the Turks on more than one occasion. And the image is indeed a reference to the Turkish Empire. Quevedo was his friend, secretary, and counsel.

IJ: "La Mosa, el Rhin, el Tajo y el Danubio."

IS: They painfully murmur his despair.

IJ: Is that how you translate *desconsuelo,* as "despair"?

IS: No, I don't like it. *Desesperación* is "despair."

IJ: "Anguish"? How about "disconsolate" or "inconsolable"?

IS: Maybe. Perhaps English doesn't have the depth of suffering to convey the true meaning.

IJ: You mentioned the adjective *baroque,* Ilan. The Spanish Golden Age is known for its baroque style. But what does the term imply?

IS: In the 1954 edition of *A Universal History of Iniquity,* Borges wrote: "I would define the baroque as that style that deliberately exhausts (or tries to exhaust) its own possibilities, and that borders on self-caricature." I like this definition. Baroque, to me, is a style that looks at itself rather than at the world. Spain's eponymous art in the seventeenth century was self-referential, to a degree of parody. Diego Velázquez's painting *Las meninas* is, in my view, the apex of baroque style.

IJ: You discuss the painting with Verónica Albin in *Love and Language* (2007).

IS: I don't want to repeat myself. However, look carefully at it: what is the viewer looking at? Himself. The painter is painting a mirror, but the viewer is standing in the place where the painter should be. In other words, whatever we see is a mirage. *Don Quixote* is another wonderful example of *lo barroco.* Even though it's an open book, it is constantly making references to itself. The interests in the roots of language that this epoch manifested aren't accidental; Spanish reached an extraordinary degree of development. In our present time, Cuban authors like Alejo Carpentier, José Lezama Lima, and Guillermo Cabrera Infante have pushed the baroque style to new heights.

IJ: In a conversation called "God's Translators" (2008) with Verónica Albin, you discussed the number of different words used by the authors of the Bible as well as by Shakespeare. Do we know how many different words Cervantes used in *Don Quixote*?

IS: It must have a total of over 425,000 words altogether.

IJ: How large was Cervantes's lexicon? In other words, how many different words did he use in the novel?

IS: I don't know. Shakespeare used around sixteen thousand. They were contemporaries. But that doesn't mean the depth of their vocabulary was equal.

IJ: Let's go back to Nebrija. His *Gramática* isn't a lexicon, though.

IS: No, it isn't. That touchstone goes to Sebastián de Covarrubias. His *Tesoro de la lengua castellana o española*—published in 1611, almost in between the publication of parts 1 and 2 of *Don Quixote of La Mancha*—is a dictionary on which future Hispanic lexicography was built. Indeed, the current edition of the *Diccionario de la lengua española de la Real Academia Española* and all its ancestors, is based on Covarrubias. This is troublesome, given that Covarrubias's effort had the imprimatur of the Holy Office of the Inquisition.

IJ: How is this manifested?

IS: Every dictionary is a product of its age. Covarrubias's objectivity is nowhere to be found. Lexicography for him is not a science but an ideological tool.

IJ: You said that Covarrubias's *Tesoro* was a touchstone.

IS: It is the foundation on which the *Diccionario de autoridades* was built. And the influence of the *Diccionario de autoridades,* published between 1729—the year the Treaty of Seville was signed between Great Britain, France, and Spain, ending the Anglo-Spanish War—and 1736, cannot be overestimated. This lexicological endeavor is less ideologically driven, even though Spaniards were aware that France had already beaten them with their dictionary by the Academie Française, a fact that prompted them to act swiftly in order not to fall far behind. Furthermore, lexicography isn't a science in Spanish with the reach it has in other languages—English, German, French, and Russian, for instance.

IJ: I know you own a large library of dictionaries.

IS: When I suffer from insomnia, I spend the hours jumping from the definition offered in one volume to its equivalent in another.

IJ: That should be turned into an official sport.

IS: What dictionaries do you prefer? When do you use them? What's your view on the role dictionaries should serve in preserving the language?

IJ: I grew up on Larousse, primarily because it served both as dictionary and encyclopedia. I still use it for quick definitions and other cultural information, but to get a sense of various connotations, I rely more heavily on the dictionary of the Real Academia Española. Having said that, I use dictionaries as a last resort. I really must be entirely unsure before I go to them. I try to get the meaning of words from context, and in that respect my best dictionary, to get at some complex meanings, is literature. I tend to savor the words, and when I see them in a complex and revealing context, I learn more about them than from dictionaries. Dictionaries are useful, no doubt about it, especially when they are descriptive. I resort to them to find out the standard usage and, to a more limited extent, what the etymology of a word might be.

IS: Usage is crucial for us in the Americas, since there is a wide range of options when it comes to Spanish in the Americas. I'm always intrigued by the way people from different countries, upon meeting each other, spend a generous portion of their time joking about the nuances of language, the fact, for instance, that the word *concha* has one meaning in the region of Argentina and Uruguay, "cunt," and a different one in Mexico, a type of pastry.

IJ: I treasure Spanish, on account of the reservoir of historical experience it provides, its ability to communicate with people across many boundaries, and its vitality, as proven by ever-more powerful writings in fiction, history, and just about every field. I would also emphasize the sheer joy of listening to it, with its sure-footed pronouncements, its musicality, its uncanny way of conveying the life of a people across the centuries. But to follow the spirit of your point, what I celebrate is its adaptability to changing situations. Certainly, Spanish doesn't have the monopoly of this particular quality, but without understanding its appeal and survival among millions of people around the world, there is no way to appreciate its gift to adapt to changing circumstances.

IS: One of the important philologists who studied that adaptability was Ángel Rosenblat. He paid attention to the varieties across the continent. I'm reminded of George Bernard Shaw's observation that Britain and the United States were "two nations divided by a common language." I sometimes think the same of the Hispanic world:

a region of more than 400 million people divided by a common language.

IJ: How about Amado Alonso?

IS: An admirable philologist, although his book *El problema de la lengua en América,* published in 1935, makes me cringe.

IJ: Why?

IS: To begin with, he sees the differences in language across the continent as a problem. In my eyes, those differences aren't a problem but a solution.

IJ: How so?

IS: I wouldn't want everyone to speak the same way. Alonso had the disease that affects numerous Spaniards: they look at the former colonies in linguistic terms as a degenerative development, not as a regenerative one. Alonso's colleague, Ramón Menéndez Pidal, with whom he worked in Madrid's Centro de Estudios Históricos, had a similar approach. Moreover, Iberian lexicography remains reactive rather than proactive. It feels as if it's always several steps behind what society is doing. And it's dismissive of the dramatic changes of Spanish in the United States, looking at them as if they were solely the result of a clashing of codes. They are much more . . .

IJ: What are they?

IS: Nowhere in the globe is Spanish experiencing more changes than in the United States. The future of the language, and its civilization, will be defined by these changes. I should say that I'm not unhappy only with the reaction in Spain. In the United States too the appreciation of this drama is slooooooooow.

IJ: How so?

IS: For one thing, nowadays Spanish in the United States is still taught as a foreign language. But is it? For years I've advocated an alternative approach. Indeed, I'm convinced that it should be taught as a native language.

IJ: What's the difference?

IS: Teaching Spanish as a foreign language asks students to perceive it as vehicle of communication that is distant, unrelated to them, like Latvian, Swahili, and Mandarin. But Spanish is an integral part of at least 15 percent of the nation's overall population. There are substantial parts of the country, from Los Angeles to Miami, where it has equal status with English or maybe even more prominence. I propose teaching Spanish as the language the student will use not only when going abroad but also in domestic traveling.

IJ: How should the pedagogical strategies in the classroom change?

IS: Spanish should be taught as part of American studies. Or in ethnic studies. In the classroom the student should perceive the Hispanic world as an organic whole that spans from San Sebastián in Spain to Ciudad Juárez on the U.S.-Mexico border, from the Argentine Pampa to New York City's Spanish Harlem.

IJ: Would that be enough—teaching Spanish from another locus?

IS: It's a start. How you teach a subject depends on where you're positioned as a thinker. But the knowledge of the history of Spanish needs to be far better known by the whole society. How come PBS has never aired a show about its development? The subject would be appealing to a large audience, don't you think?

IJ: I agree. Something equivalent to Robert MacNeil's *The Story of English* (1986).

IS: Yet Spanish, as a language, is perceived as having no history. It's seen as a kitchen language, spoken by illegal, and thus illiterate, workers, as well as women and children with no culture. It has no panache whatsoever! What's your own experience hearing different types of Spanish in the United States?

IJ: I was aware of the variances of Spanish within my own country, and then when I moved to Argentina. But it was only in the United States that I became acquainted with the smorgasbord of pronunciations and usages of Spanish. It was a liberating experience, knowing that I could still understand the general outlines and soon enjoy the musicality of words and sentences. Spanish can be, but is not always, literal. So hearing wordplay, tongue twisters, and proverbs of different types coming from different national cultures was and has always been a joy.

IS: Did this have a negative impact on you?

IJ: It kept me grounded on the Spanish matrix, just as I was trying to learn English. When I felt comfortable enough in English, the challenge was different: how not to lose Spanish fluency, especially in the U.S. Midwest, where I lived continuously for sixteen years and where much less Spanish is heard. Still, there was some. Travel and reading were also fundamental to maintaining the language. Otherwise, there's too much interference, and one begins to impose English structures and false cognates into Spanish.

IS: I understand your need to protect your Spanish. I, on the other hand, enjoy that interference. It's at the core of Spanglish . . .

IJ: Surely, though you speak as a scientist.

IS: What's your view on Spanglish?

IJ: I love it when the integrity of the two languages is maintained, which might be an oxymoron when it comes to Spanglish. That is, I love it when I hear it in thoroughly bilingual people, who switch languages with total ease, always searching for the best way to say something, regardless of language. When I read Pedro Pietri, or when I listen to the lyrics of *The Capeman,* with Rubén Blades and Marc Anthony singing along with others in the cast, I celebrate the way the two languages dance with each other. I grow less comfortable when I hear someone call me back in the literal translation "Te llamo pa'atrás," which makes no sense in Spanish. And yet it is a reality that some of these words and expressions are legitimate and comprehensible for vast numbers of people. Just on those grounds, we ought to not only watch but even encourage its full development. But, Ilan, you have written about it and compiled a whole lexicon of Spanglish words, so correct me on this.

IS: It's not a matter of correcting you! It would be ridiculous to suggest that Spanglish is a neutral phenomenon when the sole mention of the word generates deep and conflicted reactions. As far as I'm concerned, Spanglish is a natural step in the development of language.

IJ: What language?

IS: In this case, it's a step in the development of three languages: Spanish, English, and Spanglish. No language, no matter how healthy it seems, is ever static. It's in constant change, facing challenges from within and from outside its environment. The Spanish spoken in the United States today by more than forty million people is a chapter in the history of the Spanish language from Gonzalo de Berceo to Antonio Muñoz Molina and beyond. Likewise, it is part of the vitality of English. And it is shaping up to become a form of communication with its own idiosyncrasy.

IJ: Will this idiosyncrasy evolve to become a full-fledged language?

IS: I don't know. I can't read the future. What I do know is that Spanglish is enormously useful today on the street, in education, politics, and business. Does one need more proof of its vibrancy?

IJ: What is its impact on Spanish?

IS: At the very least, it keeps proud Spanish speakers in a state of constant vigilance. That defensive attitude affects the way people perceive its tongue.

IJ: How so?

IS: If you're constantly on the defense, you end up endorsing a worldview defined by vulnerability.

IJ: Are you saying that even Spanish speakers who have little contact with Spanglish are reacting to it?

IS: Of course. What we've learned in the last decades is that a sip of coffee in a Starbucks contributes to an avalanche in the Himalayas.

IJ: Do you think Spanish orthography needs to be streamlined?

IS: For one of the international congresses of the Spanish language, organized by the Real Academia de la Lengua, Gabriel García Márquez proposed simplifying the grammar of Spanish.

IJ: Actually, I was flabbergasted that García Márquez did not say that his proposal had already been advanced by Andrés Bello, Juan García del Río, and Domingo Faustino Sarmiento in the nineteenth century. Nothing in it was new. When I read the story in the *New York Times,* I wanted to write the proverbial response that would never be published, and also give him the benefit of the doubt, but in the end I concluded that he wouldn't care less about the people who actually fought for such reforms at a time when it was not simply quaint or attention-getting. He should have mentioned that the proposal was not new and that it represented a significant part of Latin American cultural and linguistic efforts following independence. But maybe he doesn't know.

IS: The question of how Spanish should be standardized has political implications.

IJ: Especially when a Latin American is behind that proposition.

IS: Spaniards dislike it when someone in Latin America recommends emendations to their tongue. They like to be perceived as the owners of Nebrija's language.

IJ: Even though they are only about forty million . . .

IS: Out of more than 400 million Spanish speakers worldwide.

IJ: Perhaps they feel that it belongs to them because the Iberian Peninsula was the cradle of Spanish.

IS: What are your own views on standard Spanish?

IJ: It is quite convenient to have the same orthography throughout the Spanish-speaking world.

IS: It isn't the case with English, although the differences are small.

IJ: It is certainly more neutral. If Colombians and Argentines had different spelling systems, which one would they use when writing to each other? If I write consistently in my national system, regardless of the systems of others, wouldn't I risk being insensitive to someone, somewhere? What is clear is that the tendency among our countries has been to communicate in a standard version, at least for the written part of our language. But it would be insane, and counterproductive, to try to impose standard Spanish in its spoken form. That isn't how language evolves and behaves in reality.

IS: Language, like nature, should run its own course.

IJ: I'm not sure, Ilan. Orality is much more malleable and allows us to convey the messages we want in ways that the standard form cannot. But written language is something else altogether. Besides, nature and language are different creatures.

IS: They are: language is human made.

IJ: Thus, constantly affected by humans.

IS: Still, I find it preposterous every time the Spanish government announces a concerted effort to salvage Spanish in the United States. How could it do it?

IJ: I don't know.

IS: I don't know either. It goes without saying that the U.S. government has an entirely different approach. But is it to salvage the Spanish language? Not, not really. To use it to advance knowledge, perhaps. But for better or worse, it has no invested interest in the durability of the language.

IJ: Yet Spanish is alive and well in colleges and universities.

IS: Ah, therein a topic I don't believe we can ignore: the role of Spanish departments in the United States in spreading the gospel of la hispanidad.

IJ: I have seen different approaches, but to this day I remain skeptical of the U.S. Department of Education proficiency standards, which many universities use, about the sequence from oral to written proficiency. It is a good thing to understand what you hear, but you cannot advance in the language, any language, unless you understand its internal logic, and that means grammar. But most universities are reluctant to teach grammar before the third year. That isn't good enough. It fosters a simplistic view of the language as a basic communications tool and not as a gateway to higher levels of understanding. The latter is supposed to happen almost automatically when students begin to read literary sources.

IS: The Real Academia Española is an organization for which I see limited need. It legislates, of course. Its motto is *Limpia, fija y da esplendor* (It cleans, establishes, and adds luster). It publishes a fine prescriptive dictionary.

IJ: Prescriptive?

IS: It tells people how to speak.

IJ: What other options are there?

IS: A descriptive dictionary like the *Oxford English Dictionary* doesn't prescribe anything.

IJ: How did you come to this conclusion?

IS: Because the *Diccionario de la lengua española de la Real Academia Española* excludes words it doesn't want people to use. A descriptive dictionary would never do that.

IJ: Mine is just a mundane perception of the Real Academia Española in Madrid, but I hope it says something. I have been to many archives in many countries, a few quite idiosyncratic, but none as impenetrable as that of the Real Academia. I went there seeking the files of some American Hispanists, but there was no way to get in! I went around the building and found one gate. But there was no bell, no hours posted for visitors and researchers, nothing. It was a most disconcerting feeling. The only way to get access is by writing to them, and even then they want to know what information you seek. Then they send it if you are lucky enough to know exactly what you want. At that point, you wonder if something was missed or badly transcribed. An academy, it seems to me, should be open to anyone with a bona fide research project, as most academies are. That sort of bunker mentality, I am sad to say, does not reflect well on their approach to language issues. If a privileged few can enter, fine for them, but they will still be the privileged few, selected by the academy itself.

IS: Talk to me about Chilean Spanish.

IJ: Andrés Bello was the first to note that it was quite atrocious. He noted how Chileans seemed to delight in murdering words, chopping off their endings, speaking in shrill tones and in unfinished, unclear sentences. I am afraid not much has changed. I would only add that gestures, onomatopoeic renditions of expressions, and whistles are regular substitutes for words. Chile does not have a monopoly on this sort of communication, but it is quite accentuated. Chilean Spanish also relies very heavily on obscenities to punctuate just about everything that is said.

IS: How has Spanish changed in Chile since you were little?

IJ: Not a whole lot, except that the vocabulary seems to have shrunk, using more Anglicisms and more obscenities. The young would never have dared to use them in conversation with an adult or when talking to the opposite sex. But now it is the rule.

IS: What kind of Spanish is used in Chilean radio and TV?

IJ: Very formal, most of the time. Recently I was interviewed by a prominent communications personality. I got to the studio a bit early, so that I had a chance to talk to him informally. To my surprise he used the common obscenity *huevón* as every other word in his sentences. But as soon as we went on the air, he reverted to a most beautiful, polished, obscenity-free Spanish.

IS: How about the Spanish used by Chilean politicians?

IJ: Same thing: formal, but quite capable of reverting to the dirtiest and most atrocious idioms when off the record. There is still some wonderful rhetoric among the older politicians, but that seems to be on the way out these days.

IS: How did your love for the language materialize?

IJ: I discovered a facility to recite poems very early on, in grammar school, or maybe I was simply drafted to do the weekly patriotic recitations before the students because no one else wanted to do the job. But I was very lucky that one teacher took special care to teach me poetry and coached me on how to recite from memory. Little by little I grew fond of the richness of the language. So, naturally, I also fell in love with writing. The usual thing: I kept a diary, wrote a poem here and there, or crafted an inscription to celebrate someone in the family. By the age of thirteen, I knew that my passion was in writing. This was not a realization about the *Spanish* language necessarily. When you are monolingual, which was certainly my case, you are like a fish in the water: unaware that there is anything beyond the water. Still, I relished all having to do with writing, experimenting with words and constructing imaginary dialogues. In the politicized sixties, when I was a secondary school student, I became the recording secretary for the student government, which meant collecting and arranging different voices in one narrative. In college, I ventured into creative writing and had my first experience with publication. But then came the military coup of 1973 and, with it, the inability to freely express my thoughts and opinions. I continued to write, however, both to keep a record of the repression and to hold on to a sense of self before a crumbling world. But I was dimly aware about what *Spanish* had to do with it all, until I was compelled to learn a new language, English, to function in my new environment in the United States. All the nuances of Spanish that I had learned, in interaction with the events of my country, had to be put on hold. I threw myself into English at age twenty-two and have never abandoned my love for this acquired language. But Spanish has always been my language, even though after thirty years I lost fluency and had to face the fact that my lexicon had become gradually fossilized and obsolete. When I returned to Chile in 2006, I embraced Spanish wholeheartedly once again, but I am still a sort of linguistic Rip Van Winkle, feeling that I have missed quite a lot.

IS: How much can Spanish change or vary?

IJ: Well, there is standard versus colloquial, or dominant versus provincial and local, as well as the marked difference in vocabulary and pronunciation among national variants. It is truly wonderful to travel to different Spanish-speaking countries and engage in conversation with people, to realize that we are communicating through different versions of Castilian Spanish and still understanding each other. I can see a place for a standard Spanish, but the joys of communication are in discovering what people mean by different expressions. I fondly remember our ride together down the Chilean coastal valley of Casablanca, on our way to Neruda's house in Isla Negra, when I confessed my failure to find a local equivalent to *Malinche* and *malinchismo,* as the feelings of national betrayal and lack of patriotism are often called in Mexico. Switching topics a bit, I want you to reflect on the Instituto Cervantes in Spain. I read a column you wrote in *El Diario* in New York calling it *"una institución apostólica."*

IS: Modeled after the Alliance Française and the Goethe-Institut, its mission is manifestly evangelical: to spread the gospel of la hispanidad, albeit from the neocolonial perspective of contemporary Spain, because Spain, unlike the countries of Latin America, is able to invest money in education and the arts. That investment is designed to present all manifestations of la hispanidad as offshoots of the Iberian civilization. In short, the Instituto Cervantes is a twenty-first-century cultural machine of regurgitating echoes.

IJ: Aren't you being harsh?

IS: Maybe I'm too soft.

IJ: The Instituto Cervantes designs its activities as a way to promote Hispanic civilization.

IS: Does it really need promoting? And what kind of Hispanic civilization do they promote? Do they invite pregnant teenagers to speak? Drug traffickers?

IJ: What type of Spanish do you think will be spoken in the twenty-second century?

IS: No matter what it is, it will be thoroughly colored—that is, restructured—by the English language. What do you think?

IJ: It will sound surprisingly close to what it is today, except that I envision more and more borrowed idioms. A language like Spanish has proven to be quite resilient. If you compare sixteenth-century English with today's version, you will probably need a course to brush up. Not so with Spanish. Calderón, Lope de Vega, and Cervantes would not be strangers in any Spanish-speaking country today.

IS: I'm not sure, Iván. Is it true that reading Shakespeare today is harder than reading Quevedo? Maybe a bit more. Does that mean that English develops at a faster speed?

IJ: Probably.

IS: Then the development of Spanglish is proof that Spanish has entered a new time zone.

IJ: Talking about how the meaning of words can change, sometimes abruptly, I remember with horror the time when one of the members of the Chilean military junta described as *humanoides* those who were Communists and therefore the enemies of the values of Western civilization. The problem for most of us, Communist or not, was that we could easily fall in this perverse trap: if you disagreed with the military government, you were (1) an enemy of Western civilization, (2) a Communist, and, ergo, (3) subhuman. And if you were that far beyond the pale of humanity, you had no protections, no rights; in fact, you were a leper, a nuisance or threat to be disposed of. As a young man, when I heard this, I naturally rebelled, with dire consequences for my safety and for the subsequent course of my life. But I learned my lesson: words should not be taken lightly. That cavalier characterization, meaningless in itself and already forgotten, reflected in a real way what some of those guys thought of us, and explains—though it does not justify—what they did. If you examine some cases beyond Chile, *Jew* or *Kurd* would have a similar meaning.

IS: Do you have a couple of Spanish words that have defined you?

IJ: Going back in time, I cannot imagine stronger or more influential and powerful expressions than Sarmiento's "civilization and barbarianism" or Bello's "freedom and license." Sarmiento celebrated "civilization" because he wanted to condemn dictatorships as forms of "barbarianism," and, in particular, the Rosas dictatorship, with all its persecutions and brutal killings. But the expression acquired a life of its own, and today many people think that Sarmiento was belittling the downtrodden in favor of an aristocracy of letters. Maybe to some extent, but his *Facundo* was primarily a condemnation of dictatorship, from an exile who latched on to a powerful dichotomy to make his point. Similarly, Bello wanted to emphasize that freedom in all areas (political and literary, in particular) did not mean that anything goes, that true liberty means rules and respect for the freedom of others. He succeeded, though in ways too subtle to fully measure how important it was, in a period of nation building, to establish that fundamental principle. On a more personal note, I was shocked to learn that descendants of *chilotes*—the people of Chiloé, as I was—were rather derogatorily called *chumangos*. I could not get it out of my head. Much later, I was amused to hear a friend call me a *chigrín,* by which he meant a *chileno-gringo,* on account of my utter inability, after thirty years, to immediately differentiate between a joke and a serious statement (I erred on the side of the latter most times, with embarrassing results), meet deadlines, and show up on time. But in Chile today, that is what I am. If I ever write a memoir, I should probably call it "From Chumango to Chigrín." How about you?

IS: I have scores of words but don't want to needlessly take your time. Let me invoke a single one that is at the core of who I am: *judío.* Sebastián de Covarrubias's *Tesoro,* about which we talked in our first conversation, offers a biased definition.

IJ: What does it say?

IS: "En la palabra hebrea tenemos dicho en qué forma aquel pueblo, que Dios escogió para sí, se llamaron hebreos y después israelitas, y finalmente judíos. Hoy día lo son los que no creyeron en la venida de Mesías Salvador, Cristo Jesús, Señor nuestro, y continúan el profesar la ley de Moisés, que era sobra desta verdad." A loose translation: "The Hebrew word implies the way that such a people, chosen by God, called itself the Hebrews, later the Israelites, and finally the Jews. Today they are those who did not believe in the coming of the Redeeming Messiah, Jesus Christ, Our Lord, and continue to profess the law of Moses, as if it were the sole truth." Thus, the beginning of Covarrubias's definition. He proceeds to offer a history of the Jewish presence in Spain, up to the use of symbols in their clothing in order to be identified as such.

IJ: Does it offend you?

IS: Not really. Being perceived as an interloper is my cross. I rather enjoy it . . .

IJ: To conclude this conversation, I want to ask you a semantic question, Ilan, and then return to a comment I made before. Why talk about *la* hispanidad and not simply about hispanidad?

IS: To me there's an intrinsic feminine quality in the concept, and the article *la* emphasizes that quality.

IJ: Also, I asked you earlier why you were not capitalizing the *h.* You responded that if the *h* is capitalized, the concept would appear to be an ideological banner.

IS: Indeed, and if there's an uppercase *H,* then the *L* in the article also needs to be capitalized. A question like "What is Hispanidad?" while grammatically correct, looks too ominous to me, too pompous.

IJ: Should we call the book with these conversations "What is la hispanidad?"

IS: Somehow the lowercase inserts a modicum of humility. Instead, I see it as a kaleidoscopic lens through which the world is perceived in different ways, depending on how one rotates the cylinder.

IVÁN JAKSIĆ: What do you think of Frida Kahlo's painting *Las dos Fridas?*

ILAN STAVANS: It is melodrama metastasized into art. Made in 1939, it depicts the painter in her two personas: the indigenous and the cosmopolitan. Their dresses establish the difference, but their hearts unite them. While their facial expressions are identical, one is a weaker Frida and the other one with the stronger heart needs to pump blood in order to keep her alive. The clouds in the background are ominous. What does the indigenous Frida hold in her left hand? Half a seed. The other Frida, instead, has a pair of surgical pincers to stop the blood drain. Is their relationship that of parasites? In any event, the painting is a superb depiction of womanhood in the Hispanic world: bleeding yet stoic.

IJ: "Bleeding yet stoic." I like the statement.

IS: Isn't that what Eva Perón is like in the photographs of her embraced by posterity? There is, no doubt, another model: Jennifer Lopez. The best word I have for her is *altanera.*

IJ: Translation?

IS: "Defiant," maybe? Not too long ago I read an insightful essay on her buttocks. The size of her bottom and the way she moves it around in her concerts makes it an object of adoration in the Caribbean Basin. To what extent is her bottom a symbol of Puerto Ricanness? I imagine comedian John Leguizamo using it as the inspiration for a skit in which he personifies a Japanese businessman giving a lecture to Latinos about giving up the greasy food, the body fat, in order to achieve a successful crossover in the business world. Jennifer Lopez, part black, part Puerto Rican, is *the* model of success, her buttocks and all.

IJ: Aren't there various models of *feminidad?*

IS: No doubt. Octavio Paz, in *The Labyrinth of Solitude,* talks of the extremes: the virgin and the prostitute.

IJ: Feminists thoroughly dislike Paz, as you know. They view *The Labyrinth of Solitude* as misogynistic. Jean Franco, for instance, suggests that Paz's reading of Sor Juana Inés de la Cruz's oeuvre in *The Traps of Faith* is misguided, never stressing enough the forces that defined her as a female poet in colonial Mexico.

IS: And well they should.

IJ: As you suggested, in this sixth conversation let's focus on media representations.

IS: A quick, superficial look at TV images of Spanish-language channels in the United States evidences the obvious: Univision traffics in syrupy melodrama. Flipping through the channels, the viewer doesn't have to know Spanish to recognize a *telenovela.* This recognition happens anywhere in the world. In the United States, non-Latinos become acquainted with Hispanic civilization through these narratives.

IJ: Where does it come from?

IS: Hispanic melodrama has its roots in mid-twentieth-century romantic serials (novels and other fictions) in newspapers and magazines, such as the work of Corín Tellado, the pen name of María del Socorro Tellado López, born in 1927 in Viavélez, Asturias, in Spain. She has published more than four thousand novels and sold more than 400 million books, which have been translated into several languages. In the Guinness World Records, Corín Tellado is listed as the author who has sold the most books written in the Spanish language.

Her forgettable style has antecedents. In the second half of the nineteenth century, writers of lowbrow lineage would include Benito Pérez Galdós, the so-called Iberian Charles Dickens, as well as Leopoldo Alas (a.k.a. Clarín) and Emilia Pardo Bazán. But the right ancestry has less to do with novels than with *fotonovelas,* melodramatic stories told in comic-book format through photographs.

IJ: I do remember seeing those coveted issues on kiosks all over town in the Santiago of my youth. Not all could afford them, for they were somewhat expensive. But how they passed from hand to hand!

IS: The question is what cultural capital do Latin American soaps have. My response: an insurmountable one. In the Mexico of my adolescence, everybody would interrupt their daily routine to watch the end of a serial. And I'm not talking only about the lower and middle classes. Government offices could close early to give people enough time to have dinner and be happily positioned in front of their TV screen before the prime-time episode was about to air. Patrons and maids, doctors, nurses, and patients, teachers and students . . . *todo el mundo* got involved. At one point, even the nation's president postponed an important speech so as not to overlap with (and have a disadvantage against) the conclusion of a *telenovela*. I was in my late teens, I believe, when the format changed somewhat: from serials that could last several years, producers moved to a shorter, more contained narrative of approximately forty to sixty chapters. And the emphasis changed too. The ones I used to watch were always about a set of contemporary issues; race, class, and sexuality were the central themes. But in my twenties, more historically minded soaps began to air, about canonical figures in the nation's past like the independence leaders Father Miguel Hidalgo y Costilla and José María Morelos y Pavón and their nemesis, the thirty-year-plus dictator Porfirio Díaz, though of course they weren't contemporaries.

IJ: So they do serve a didactic purpose. Do they help in providing a sense of who we are culturally and historically?

IS: The *telenovela* is an enormous machine that promotes the concept of la hispanidad in a subliminal fashion. Think of it as an endless quantity of kitsch with a message.

IJ: What kind of message?

IS: That Hispanic civilization is about overwrought emotions. Also, that loyalty and hypocrisy are the essential feelings defining it. In every Latin American soap there's a sequence of secrets keeping the plot moving: Does the rich, handsome man really love the gorgeous maid? Is the child she's about to have illegitimate? Will her brother take revenge?

IJ: So they capture something that may not be on the radar screen of intellectuals. But is this expression of emotions, at least as portrayed by the media, unique to us?

IS: Emotions are expressed in Mediterranean cultures in extroverted form.

IJ: Your father, I understand, is a soap opera actor.

IS: Yes, for years he has worked for Televisa, the major private TV corporation in Mexico. When I was little, I would accompany him to the studio. He performed a variety of roles, then and later, in serials like *Simplemente María, No todo lo que brilla es oro, Pelusita,* and *La sonrisa del diablo.*

IJ: Did you ever act?

IS: Actually, I did a couple of roles as an extra. To call them cameos would elevate them to a status they didn't have. I mostly appeared in the background, as filler. I remember a scene at a restaurant. A friend of mine and I were asked to go through the door of the place as the lead couple was leaving the place. On another occasion, I actually had a speaking role—of three words. And I couldn't deliver them in a natural way. We did half a dozen reshots, maybe more. You see, in Mexican *telenovelas* actors use *el aparato,* an earphone that tells them what to say a second before they have to deliver the line.

IJ: You wrote about it in *On Borrowed Words.*

IS: It was extraordinarily difficult for me to concentrate. I was sixteen or seventeen at the time.

IJ: Did the experience change you in any way?

IS: Not really. What I learned is to understand the cultural value of soaps. Latin America can't take credit for inventing new artistic genres—other than the *telenovela.* In Russia, Greece, Korea, and other countries, the Mexican soap in particular has an unending popularity. Not too long ago, I was in Israel, where a large portion of the population, especially those between fifteen and thirty years of age, was watching serials like *La vengadora* with religious devotion. And I'm not using the adjective *religious* lightly for a region where fanaticism comes in all shapes and forms. Indeed, an entire generation has learned Spanish through the *telenovela.* Such is the passion that the genre awakens that the young, after finishing their army service (in their mid-twenties), travel for a year in Mexico, Central America, Colombia, Bolivia, and other places in Latin America, a year of distancing from the hypermilitarized life they have been living.

IJ: The cultural implications, then, are truly enormous, quite beyond the original intentions of the *telenovelas* themselves.

IS: Pedro Almodóvar, the superb Spanish filmmaker, has taken the genre of the *telenovela* to a new level.

IJ: It is marvelous when it works well.

IS: Iván, your opinion on *telenovelas?*

IJ: There is much of the rationalist in me that has always prevented me from enjoying them or even appreciating them as artifacts of popular culture. I have found them always too histrionic, overacted, and in most ways simplistic. But I admire the suspense, which remind me of the *folletines*, newspaper serials of the nineteenth century.

IS: Is there a film or films that had a *personal* impact on you?

IJ: After I left Argentina and Chile, I arrived in the States with a heavy baggage of repressed emotions. Having escaped arrest, having lived through moments of intense violence and utter terror, as well as experiencing anger and impotence when going through government offices and detention centers to locate friends, I was in my own state of denial when I reached the United States. I struggled to be like a normal graduate student, but my psychological state was really quite precarious, and it was bound to break down when faced with representations of what I had recently experienced. The first time it happened was at the State University of New York's student union cinema, as I watched *Madame Rosa,* with Simone Signoret in the lead role. Never mind that it was about the Nazis and about a time that seemed remote from my own. It was then and there, in 1977, that I recognized that I would never escape the memories of the fear that I had lived in Chile and Argentina.

IS: Watching a movie at the right time can change one's life.

IJ: There is a scene in which, many years after the occupation, Madame Rosa still calmly gathers her belongings, fully expecting to be picked up to go to prison, clearly captive to her memories and still acting upon them. At the time, I was still sleeping on the floor, fully dressed and prepared to run. Watching the film, the boundaries between actor and audience dissolved for me, and I felt a sudden explosion in my chest, like a torrent of steam that choked my throat, pressed my temples, and made my eyes swell. I had to leave the theater to give full release to a volcano of emotions. I came face-to-face with the reality that I would never escape those memories. More than thirty years later, I know I was right. But at the same time, the film did start a process of healing for which I am grateful, though it took some seventeen years for me to first write about it and go public in my "In Search of Safe Haven." In between, two other films had a similar, though not as intense, impact on me, *Missing* and *El Norte.*

I still find the first biased and questionable, but few have conveyed so well the intensity of fear when military violence is unleashed against an unarmed civilian population. *El Norte* showed not only the same state of political terror but also the difficulties of the experience of immigration. When you have done menial jobs to survive and struggled to cope with recent memories of fear, not to mention struggled with language and a new dominant culture, you can fully appreciate that film.

IS: Are there any films that have shocked you in a different way?

IJ: I was quite offended by some depictions of Latinos in Hollywood films. *Scarface* was one of the worst, especially because I truly admired Al Pacino as an actor, and I thought that his range in portraying the Italian American experience would somehow apply to the Latino experience as well. It took me years to understand that we had just replaced the bad guys from the Cold War and would later pass the dubious baton on to Muslims. But in between we were fair game for the insulting depiction of us as drug lords and trigger-happy hoodlums.

IS: I, on the other hand, like Brian De Palma's remake of *Scarface*, although I'm puzzled by its status as a cult classic. Some among my students' generation dangerously approach it as the ultimate expression of Cuban American immigration. In any case, think of Cantinflas. His depiction of *el peladito,* a street-smart Mexican, should also offend us, don't you think? Yet it makes us laugh . . .

IJ: I know Cantinflas is one of your heroes.

IS: Cantinflas, in my view, also proposes an ingenious view of la hispanidad. What is he? A bum, a good-for-nothing. But Cantinflas has a heart. He might be poor and almost illiterate, but he knows good from evil.

IJ: You have written a substantial essay on Cantinflas and have put him in the title of a collection of essays, *The Riddle of Cantinflas.* Obviously you do see an important cultural meaning in his acting, but you also seem fascinated by the man himself and his trajectory. Who was he as an actor?

IS: Cantinflas is a by-product of the *carpa* tradition, an ambulant circus that in Mexico in the early twentieth century incorporated stand-up comedy.

IJ: So he really developed his artistry on the ground.

IS: Tin-Tan is another legendary *carpa* comedian. One day I would like to write about him. The more I watch him on YouTube and in movies, the larger my empathy is. Tin-Tan came from a family of actors. When I was an adolescent, I used to watch the TV show starring his younger brother Manuel "El Loco" Valdés, who was true to his artistic name: absolutely crazy.

IJ: But also a pioneer . . .

IS: Tin-Tan spent time with the pachucos in California. Indeed, *la pachucada* is a central component of his style. He is often dressed as a pachuco: his suit consists of baggy trousers tapered at the ankles, a knee-length jacket, a tie, a stylized hat, and a pompously greaser haircut. And his language is in permanent flux, switching from Spanish to English and back, translating expressions, using false cognates. There is an endearing scene in which he sings an idiosyncratic version the Beatles song "I Want to Hold Your Hand:" "Oh yea, dame tu mano, que tengo comezón, / Oh yea, dame tu mano, quiero rascarme aquíííí" (Oh yeah, give me your hand, because I'm itching, / Oh yeah, give me your hand, I want to scratch right here). I dream of one day writing a fully illustrated book about Tin-Tan as an archetype pachuco. Octavio Paz, in the first chapter of *The Labyrinth of Solitude,* ridicules these types as "extreme Mexicans." Paz, I'm afraid, got it all wrong: the pachuco wasn't an extreme Mexican; he was a *new* Mexican. The character of Tin-Tan uses Spanglish in a way that is far ahead of his time.

IJ: I wonder also about the emphasis on drug trafficking and natural catastrophes. It would appear that little else happens in Latin America.

IS: Or sports, the real opium of the people. Let us talk a bit about it.

IJ: The part of the world where I was born made indoor sports a necessity because of the harsh weather, so I played basketball and practiced gymnastics. There was no television at the time, so I was never swept away by soccer and played it only when I moved to Santiago, where it was indeed a passion and, for me, a way to fit in. But I was not fired up by it. Only in the States did I begin to play more seriously, even competitively, because I understood quite clearly that it was a vehicle for communication, camaraderie, and plain fun for those who play the game, at whatever level of skill. Immigrants struggle to belong, and sports serve that welcoming role, if only ephemerally, until the next game. It is like another form of communication, a physical language, as it were. But I do not mean to beg your question. What is applicable to the personal, when we discover that we can communicate with others anytime, anywhere through sports, is also applicable to countries, like my own, which strive to compete, to be on a par with the best in the world. Sports, like education, are a means to upward social mobility.

IS: Soccer—*el fútbol*—also played a crucial role in my education.

IJ: You've told a moving anecdote about it to Verónica Albin in *Love and Language*.

IS: It is hard to imagine the Hispanic world without soccer.

IJ: Impossible. Here in Santiago everyone was in tears about the death in August 2009 of Francisco "Chamaco" Valdés, a veteran of the 1962 World Cup and the country's highest international scorer. Then, in October 2009, Chile made it to the World Cup competition after defeating Colombia. The entire country seemed to go into a state of frenzy.

IS: Soccer is so significant that in my eyes la hispanidad is framed by it and not the other way around. The opiate of the people, as Eduardo Galeano asks? Not quite. The way the *hinchas* (fans) of our respective national teams passionately (or, shall I say, obsessively?) endorse (or adore?) their players is part of our weltanschauung. Think of Argentine fans, Mexicans, Uruguayans—their facial expressions, their colorful enthusiasm.

IJ: The idea of la hispanidad spilling itself out . . .

IS: Emptying itself in the stadium, on the street, at home. *El fútbol,* of course, isn't a force of change in Latin America. On the contrary, it is a mechanism through which economic, class, religious, and gender parameters are reinforced. For instance, soccer players are almost universally deprived of an ideological viewpoint. What matters to the fans is that they score a goal, not that they open their mouth to criticize the military rule in a particular country. They must be team players on the field, sacrificing their individuality, their ego even, for the good of the team. Professional clubs, corporate sponsors, and political elites throw their power behind a team and thus are perceived not only as contributing to the well-being of society but as safeguarding a parcel of the nation's collective identity.

Needless to say, the sport fosters nationalism. This is all the more apparent every four years, at the time of the World Cup.

I want to delve a bit more into the issue of sexuality. In the Hispanic world, *el fútbol* is a male sport. There are, no doubt, women's teams, and their prominence increases as time goes by. But for the time being, soccer is a training camp of masculinity. In spite of the contradiction of displaying adult men in shorts, the endeavor emphasizes physical stamina, balance, courage, handsomeness, and a shrewd positioning in the field, which in the imagination of the audience is a symbol for life in general. Players arrive on the field with a "wet look" and leave it sweaty, their uniforms occasionally splashed in mud.

IJ: These comments remind me that in *The Hispanic Condition* you talk about carnivals as the ultimate expression of la hispanidad.

IS: The carnival has its roots in the Middle Ages as an occasion to relax the social mores. Once a year the lower class would be allowed to escape its burdens by dressing up in costumes that belonged to the nobility. This custom was adopted in the Hispanic world with particular emphasis, perhaps because our moral code is too stern. In any case, the carnival—and its sibling, the parade—-is an occasion to transgress without penalty. That's why I find the holiday so appealing! Dressing up is something we do all year to pretend to be who we are, but for the carnival we hide, pretending to be someone else. It reminds me of the plight of the *conversos* in Catholic Spain: forced to be who they were not, they hid their faith from the public.

IJ: I have never been to the most famous of all, in Rio, but since Carnival is rooted in an ancient religious tradition, it is to be found everywhere, in a range of manifestations. It was in Argentina that I first experienced one and appreciated its truly popular, class-bending, and joyous chaos. The leveling of social difference is a substantial ingredient of Carnival, even though it is now quite elaborate and media-driven in its present Brazilian version.

IS: Sports does that as well. The intelligentsia seldom pay attention to it. Ever heard Borges talk about Maradona? How about Octavio Paz and Carlos Fuentes about the archrivalry between the soccer clubs América and Chivas? Too mundane a topic for them, I'm afraid. Incredible as it is, *The Labyrinth of Solitude,* which purports to explain the Mexican character, altogether ignores *el fútbol.* What nearsightedness! It's another literary tradition, the one represented by Elena Poniatowska and Carlos Monsiváis, which addresses the theme in its *crónicas*. The mantle of the tradition, with a somewhat more refined facade, is in the hands of Juan Villoro.

IJ: I do not believe that Cortázar or Donoso or indeed any of the Boom writers have been able to elevate the passions of soccer to the level of artistic creativity.

IS: I love soccer. Every four summers, when the World Cup takes place, I do nothing else except watch each of the matches. *El fútbol* is a way to let our passion run amok. As with *telenovelas*, the government knows that the sport—to use a Marxist definition—is the opiate of the masses. It offers a galaxy of heroes and villains and a channel to express one's animalistic instincts that is simultaneously democratic and nonthreatening.

IJ: The way you describe it makes it sound as if it's a way not just to integrate parts of the self but also to create a larger community.

IS: Among Latinos in the United States, *el béisbol* has a similar psychological use. People identify with teams like the Mets, the Cubs, and the Red Sox as an entryway to community. Indeed, one could understand the ups and downs of the assimilation process through baseball. Players like Jackie Robinson, Hank Greenberg, and Minnie Minoso were emblems—maybe the word is *pistons*—of integration. They greased the system so that blacks, Jews, and Latinos in general could feel less threatened as minorities.

IJ: Did you ever play distinctly Hispanic children games?

IS: Of course. For years I thought that *la rayuela,* known in English as hopscotch, was particular to Mexico. But there are multiple varieties in the world: in Persian culture—that is, in Iran—it is called *laylay;* in France, *escargot,* meaning "snail," and *la marelle ronde,* round hopscotch; in Germany (I love this version!) it is known as *Himmel und Hölle,* heaven and hell. Far more autochthonous are *la matatena, la piñata,* and *la lotería.* The last one is a particular type of lottery played with cards.

IJ: Didn't you write a book about *la lotería?*

IS: Yes, with artist Teresa Villegas. In my introductory essay I recalled playing *la lotería* in Mexico when I was a child, thinking I could control fate.

IJ: How about children's songs?

IS: "Duérmase, mi niño," "De colores" . . . To this day there's an array of specifically Mexican songs that children grow up with. It shapes our view of the world.

IJ: What makes them Mexican?

IS: A good question. They aren't patriotic. Maybe the fact that they convey *la mexicanidad.* To be honest, I wouldn't be surprised to find that these songs are ubiquitous to the Hispanic world. Did you listen to the songs of Cri-Cri when you were young?

IJ: No, but I cannot be sure that it was not available in my environment, which was so cut off from the rest of the country and region. I wouldn't dismiss it as part of our collective memory. Please define it for me.

IS: Cri-Cri (the Singing Cricket) was the pseudonym of Francisco Gabilondo Soler, who was born in Orizaba, Veracruz, in 1907 and died in Texcoco, Estado de México, in 1990. The equivalent of Raffi in the United States, Cri-Cri wrote numerous children hits: "Caminito de la escuela," "La negrita Cucurumbé," "La patita," "El chorrito," "Cochinitos dormilones," "El comal y la olla," "La merienda," and "Negrito bailarín." I once tried playing these songs for my children and was embarrassed. Interestingly, many of the song titles use the diminutive.

IJ: Why?

IS: As a form of endearment.

IJ: I have distant memories of songs that were not patriotic in my childhood. In a town with just one hundred thousand people, cut off from the rest of the country and with access to only local Chilean (and local Argentine) radio stations, I would hear the standard fare of pop songs from the United States or Europe in the form of scratchy recordings, or "ethnic" music, primarily from programs led by the local Croatian or other immigrant communities. My father deejayed a traditional Croatian music program in a local radio station for a while. Occasionally there would be a musical film, with the insufferable Joselito or Marisol from Spain. I should say, though, that I admired the latter when I saw her cameo appearance in the Carlos Saura version of *Bodas de sangre,* singing a most beautiful yet sad lullaby. Because of our proximity to Argentina, tango was big, so Carlos Gardel, Julio Sosa, and many others were very much a part of the sounds of my childhood. But so were the Beatles, and countless bolero singers who seemed to be the rage for my parents' generation. Moving to Santiago, though, I found that the dominant sounds were (in addition to the ubiquitous commercial pop) from the folklore of the central valley, with all its celebrations of agriculture and ranching. But in the sixties, those traditional *cueca* (Chile's national folk dance) and *tonada* (lighthearted song) sounds were turning into neo-folklore and protest songs.

IS: You must have grown up with *canciones de protesta,* the protest songs that became fashionable after the Cuban Revolution of 1958–1959. That, at least, was the impression we had in Mexico: Chilean children got their rebellious spirit in the milk they drank and the songs they heard.

IJ: Though it coexisted with rock, neo-folklore was very inspirational and politically motivating for my generation. There were groups, such as Quilapayún and Inti-Illimani, but there were also soloists, like Violeta Parra and Víctor Jara. Both wrote and sang some of the most beautiful lyrics of any time in Chile, but in the case of Víctor Jara I should say that he also exacerbated the political tensions that eventually would lead to tragedy, both for himself and for our country. I remember quite clearly when he released his song on the massacre at Puerto Montt, in which he made cabinet minister Edmundo Pérez Zujovic responsible for it, quite openly and defiantly. When Pérez Zujovic was assassinated by a fringe revolutionary group, it was clear that collectively we had entered a world where political violence, justified or not, had become common currency. The whole country was swept away with it, and it is unfortunate to relate the sounds of the music to the unnecessary blood that was spilled. On the whole, his music, which was not all protest, like Mercedes Sosa's in Argentina, defined a new consciousness, a new sensitivity, about our country and about our people. Sosa's death in October 2009 was sincerely mourned in Argentina and Chile. It was the end of an era.

IS: There is much to be said about Latin music as a conduit of la hispanidad.

IJ: It might well be its key promoter.

IS: Its conduit, too. Think of children's songs like "De colores" ... We used to sing it when I was little in Mexico. It has a message of unity: we Latinos are of many colors, and that multiplicity should be exalted rather than ignored or denigrated, for nature itself is also multicolored.

IJ: The more I think about it, the more I believe music is the Rorschach test for interpreting Hispanic civilization.

IS: Latin music has burst into the mainstream of American culture since the end of World War II, but especially from the eighties onward. Celia Cruz, Tito Puente, and Rubén Blades, all salseros, defined the New York music scene. Their rhythms promoted a concept of la hispanidad based on shared intrinsic values. Take the lyrics of most of Blades's songs, starting with "Pedro Navaja." His types are downtrodden Puerto Ricans, Panamanians, Mexicans, and others who struggle to survive but, in that day-to-day fight, keep their integrity and their sense of self intact. They might be thieves and prostitutes, priests and drunkards, but they persist against all odds in their mission to find meaning in life within their habitat.

IJ: The variety is so immense these days, but I am still impressed when I hear musicians combine different traditions or use established traditions to convey new messages. I will never forget a visit to Cuba in the mid-nineties, where I was given a number of recycled tapes with locally produced rock music, which turned out to be compelling protest songs. Music has been and continues to be a key form of expression, another sign of the vitality of Hispanic culture.

IVÁN JAKSIĆ: I have come to believe that we exemplify the dichotomy Isaiah Berlin suggested in his essay "The Hedgehog and the Fox" (1953), on Leo Tolstoy's theory of history, which Berlin took from a line from the Greek poet Archilochus: "The fox knows many things, but the hedgehog knows only one." I am the hedgehog, and you are the fox. I think in the end I have been more amenable to accepting a concept of la hispanidad while you have run circles around it.

ILAN STAVANS: It's good to know only one thing.

IJ: Given the question around which our discussion has rotated—what is la hispanidad?—it seems to me that while this is a concept that might be difficult to define, people, particularly those inside Hispanic civilization, know exactly what it is.

IS: And what it will be, for it seems to have a handsome future. I like the subtitle we've chosen for this small volume: "A conversation." It simultaneously describes what we've been engaged in—a dialogue—and it responds to the title's question: What is la hispanidad? It is a conversation. In other words, no strict definition of la hispanidad can ever be fully satisfying, because what we're addressing exists in a state of fluidity. The closest we might get to explaining its core meaning is through an open-ended, comprehensive discussion because—*miraculo omnium*—its meaning is nothing but a conversation.

IJ: I'm more cautious than you, Ilan. The substance is there, indeed, but several elements conspire against la hispanidad as an intellectual approach that embraces a whole range of experiences from historical to philosophical. It would seem that between the media that emphasize leftward movements, populism, drugs, and natural disasters, and an academic world that has trouble going beyond the presumed magical realism of the region, there is little room to take la hispanidad to the next intellectual level.

IS: It's important to consider the role of academia in shaping the concept. As you've put it, in U.S. universities the study of the Spanish-speaking world, in particular the Americas, dates back to the second half of the nineteenth century. To a small extent, the 1848 Treaty of Guadalupe Hidalgo, by which Mexico sold two-thirds of its territory to its northern neighbor after the Mexican-American War, initiated a process that acquired momentum by the time the Spanish-American War of 1898 was fought. Prescott, with his monumental chronicles of the conquest of Mexico and Peru, did much to generate interest. Moving forward to the present, I'm puzzled by the function of departments like those devoted to Spanish, Latin American studies, and Latino studies. And Hispanic studies.

IJ: Yes, the pioneer Hispanists did much to advance the field, though their legacy was problematic. The creation of professional higher education, in turn, brought in a whole new set of problematic issues, despite its vaunted objectivity.

IS: Take the case of Hispanic studies, an interdisciplinary field perceived as an umbrella under which Spain, the Americas, the Spanish-speaking Caribbean, and Latinos in the United States are covered.

IJ: Interdisciplinary because it encompasses history, sociology, political science, literature, et cetera.

IS: Yes. Almost nowhere in the U.S. academy are there departments of European studies. There are departments of German, Italian, et cetera. But the colonial European civilizations that reached across the Atlantic (Spain, Portugal, and France) synthesize under a single rubric a wide-range of cultures. Under Portuguese studies, students learn about Portugal and Brazil, unquestionably an ambitious undertaking. Likewise, in French studies, the culture of France is analyzed as well as that of the Francophone Caribbean. And in Hispanic studies just about everything that relates to the Spanish-speaking countries comes under a single umbrella: Spain in all its complexity, Mexico, Central America, South America, the Spanish-speaking Caribbean, and Latinos in the United States.

IJ: Could that be seen as an attempt to be inclusive, to provide keys to understand a complex subject?

IS: I return to our ongoing question: is it possible to understand

Hispanic civilization as a unit? I said earlier that it is more than the sum of its parts. But as you and I have found out, it might also be less than that. In my view, the effort at unifying such a multiheaded monster is daunting, so diverse and heterogeneous is the civilization at its core.

IJ: The United States celebrates the unity in diversity, *E pluribus unum,* but what you are saying is that it is impossible to understand the Hispanic experience without fully embracing the diversity, even if that means no unity.

IS: I've noticed that in the past few years most of the Latinos I know who are making a dent are married to people of other ethnic groups. For instance, a Latina TV producer I used to work with at WGBH, the Boston affiliate of PBS, is a Panamanian whose husband is Irish. Her boss is a Chicano from San Antonio whose spouse is Jewish and from Minnesota. The list is endless. Maybe it's the people I move with, since I too am married to a non-Latina: Alison Sparks, a psychologist and speech pathologist born in St. Louis but raised in Hartford, Connecticut.

IJ: Are you suggesting that mixed marriages are a ticket to success?

IS: Maybe that's what I'm after, although I know the idea is politically explosive. However, it does showcase a certain pattern of behavior. Mixed marriages within the Latino minority in the United States (a Cuban with a Puerto Rican, a Mexican with an Argentinean, and so on) are quite common. And also common—I'm not sure if in equal numbers—are marriages between Latinos and non-Latinos. My view is that entrance to U.S. culture is facilitated that way. I want to be careful because I'm not suggesting a programmatic approach. Perhaps in some cases the Latino partner is looking at the non-Latino potential spouse in practical ways, as a way out of a certain neighborhood and into another. But in most cases love is just love: spontaneous, irrational . . .

IJ: You meditated on the topic of love, with sensitivity, in your conversations with Verónica Albin in *Love and Language.* Although, if memory serves me well, the theme of interracial relations wasn't contemplated.

IS: You're right. *Love and Language* was about the concept of love as it changes from one civilization to another, from one historical period to the next. Yet, in the theme that concerns us, the idea is crucial. How is la hispanidad passed on from generation to generation? Through DNA? By means of family lore? What was your experience raising a child in the United States?

IJ: When my daughter was born in 1988, I already had plenty of experience seeing the children of my Chilean exile friends grow up. Some of them tried but could not quite manage to instill Chilean values in them, which usually led to alienation, conflict, and failure. Others were a bit more tolerant but grew anxious and sad when they realized that while they themselves might at some point return to their home country, their children would not. A lot of this was in the back of my mind when my daughter entered this world. Fortunately for us, it was such a joyous entrance, such a gift to our lives, that there was never any thought of anything but letting her make her own choices. I did, just in case, register her name in the Chilean consulate in San Francisco (she was born in Oakland), to give her the option of becoming a Chilean citizen when she turned eighteen (she is still considering it), but I never tried to persuade her to do it, much less to move to Chile when I finally did in 2006. But we took her often to visit the country, and to this day she enjoys coming here for short stints. My wife, Carolina, is a Mexican American from Kansas City, so it was always understood that we as a family unit had some ways, some values, that were not standard midwestern values or preoccupations (we had lived in Wisconsin and Indiana for almost my daughter's entire life). But since we were not conflicted about it, there was never an issue about our identity or hers. We always spoke Spanish at home, and that retained our Hispanic or, in my case, immigrant side. Having lived my entire adult life in the United States, I was never conflicted about having a child who was more American than Chilean, or Latin American. But as I tried to explain in "In Search of Safe Haven," those kinds of rigid boundaries, when we think about the present United States, no longer exist.

IS: My own path is different. What ties me to my wife, Alison, is empathy, and that empathy has to do with Jewishness. I was born in Mexico. She was born in the United States, and so were my two children, Joshua in 1991 and Isaiah in 1996. In the family dynamic, I'm the immigrant with the accent. That grants me an amorphous place: the outsider, the newcomer, the target of endearing jokes.

IJ: Does it make you uncomfortable?

IS: Not in the least.

IJ: Do you feel your boys have a connection with the United States that you don't have?

IS: By all means. For one thing, I don't believe in the superstition we call nationalism. I immigrated to the United States because I felt I would be able to freely express myself in this country, to thrive as a thinker. Each and every day of my life, I'm wholeheartedly proud, even grateful, for the chance to be able to say what's in my mind. But I wouldn't go to war for this country, just as I wouldn't go to war for Mexico, Israel, or any other country.

IJ: You called nationalism a superstition . . .

IS: Indeed. And I would call God another superstition. The other day I was talking to a friend of mine who is considering the rabbinate as a life career. He's an intelligent, fabulously well-read man in his early forties who has a doctorate from Columbia University. He has been president of a graduate institution and a cultural foundation and now heads his own business-consulting firm. He was debating whether to sacrifice the type of life he leads for another one in which devotion to others is the prime motif. At one point in our conversation, we stopped at the concept of sacrifice. One of us invoked the biblical story of Abraham's being asked by God to take his only son, who had come rather late in his and his wife's lives, to the top of a hill and kill him to honor the divine. Let me put it another way: Abraham must prove his commitment to God by killing, with his own hands, what he most cherishes. In the biblical passage, Abraham agrees to do as he is asked. Incredulous, Isaac asks his father what the purpose of the climb is. He is told that a sacrifice will take place, so he asks where the sacrificial animal is. His father responds that the animal will be there in due time. But just as the killing of Isaac is about to take place, an angel intercedes.

IJ: God changes His mind.

IS: He does, certainly. Still, for me the episode proves how cruel the biblical God can be. Anyhow, Abraham is ready to complete his task! As a father, I would *never* be able to do the same.

IJ: You italicized the word *never*.

IS: If I could, I would underline it and put it in bold, all at the same time.

IJ: What did your friend think of the story?

IS: He has three children: two daughters and a son. I asked him if he would be ready to do as Abraham had. He said no but added that if his nation made the same request, he would not hesitate. Rather than a rabbi, then, he should become a politician. That kind of superstition is crucial when it comes to securing votes.

IJ: I take your point about the extremes of belief or patriotism, but the Latino minority in the United States seems to me to be quite patriotic.

IS: I have no doubt. That's why, when I hear someone questioning the commitment to assimilation by Latinos, I cringe. The percentage of Mexicans and Puerto Ricans killed in the Iraq War is high. The number of Latinos who died on September 11, 2001, is also substantial. They were janitors, waiters, technicians, window cleaners, police officers, and firefighters in New York. Not part of the upper crust who worked at stock companies but an essential component of the infrastructure that kept the city moving every day.

IJ: Why wouldn't this be sufficiently recognized? How does that make you feel, as an immigrant?

IS: I often have dreams about not fitting in, of being a pariah. In one recent dream I was at a zoo. A crowd congregated around the lion's cage, looking at the lion eating a piece of meat. I attempted to find a place where I could also see, but people, in a subtle fashion, pushed me away. Then I got a chair. Maybe a guard had used it, but he or she was somewhere else and the chair was empty. I stood on the chair and looked above everyone, only to realize it wasn't the lion that was eating meat but the panther that was devouring the lion. I was shocked!

IJ: You must tell me what this means, because we combine so many elements of life and experience in our dreams, without referring directly to our day-to-day experience.

IS: I don't know what it means, Iván. But I know how it feels. Bishop Berkeley once spoke about the nature of dreams. He said, wisely, that we don't dream up a panther and then experience fear; rather, we experience fear and then dream up a panther.

IJ: Do you dream in Spanish?

IS: I'm frequently asked that question. I'm afraid my answer will not satisfy you, though. In my dreams I don't hear people speak, although I see them moving their mouths, engaging in a dialogue, understanding what others say, et cetera. In other words, my dreams, unfortunately, are languageless.

IJ: Only on the surface . . .

IS: They also don't come with subtitles!

IJ: In my case, I knew that I had turned a corner when I first dreamed in English, some two years into my life in the United States. The situation was purely parochial, like some exchange at the university library or in a market or store. But it meant the world to me. I knew that the fear that had haunted me after leaving Chile had receded, that the normal had reclaimed its space in my consciousness. Fortunately, I have always been meticulous about registering thoughts and experiences, but a review of my recorded dreams tells me primarily about specific people I cared about and relationships.

IS: One day I would like to write a world history of dreams. Or maybe I should be more modest: a personal history of dreams.

IJ: You said at the beginning of our conversations that each civilization dreams in a different way.

IS: I'm sure that's the case.

IJ: You must recall Philip K. Dick's similarly suggestive title, *Do Androids Dream of Electric Sheep?* (1968). In the same vein, how do people in Hispanic civilization dream?

IS: It's a fascinating question. I'm not sure, because, like everyone else, I am only able to dream my own dreams. But when others describe their dreams to me, certain patterns become apparent.

IJ: Such as?

IS: Well, for one thing, dreams are inspired, though not exclusively, by our immediate experience. There are no scientific studies I know of addressing the topic, but I believe there is a grammar of dreams. Sigmund Freud believed that dreams are an expression of the inner forces that define our sexuality. The tension between our impulses, the social mores that surround us, and the way our personality negotiates the two sides—that is, the barbaric versus the civilized—is expressed in the narratives we dream of every night, even though we might not remember those narratives the moment we wake up. Carl Gustav Jung, instead, was convinced that more ancient, mythical messages are delivered through our dream life, messages dealing with spiritual concerns that have been part of humanity since the beginning.

I believe there is a third component: the metabolism of the civilization the person belongs to emerges in dreams. People in the Hispanic world are exposed to raw emotions in a way some other cultures are not.

IJ: Are you saying that emotions in our dreams are displayed differently?

IS: I'm perfectly aware that I'm speaking about a terra incognita. I don't have a way to prove this argument, because I'm no psychologist, although I do have a license to practice as one.

IJ: You do?

IS: Yes. When I was seventeen, I told my father I wanted to become an artist—if not a writer, maybe a filmmaker. As an actor, he didn't try to dissuade me. But he knew how difficult it was for an actor like him to support a family of five. So he drafted a contract with me. He promised to help me in times of trouble—should I need the help and ask for it—if I got a degree in a discipline I would be able to use in case my artistic career reached a dead end. I complied happily, making psychology my choice.

IJ: Then you *are* a psychologist.

IS: Maybe. But I don't think of myself as one. Anyhow, imagine for a second that Robinson Crusoe had a child on the island where he lived in Daniel Defoe's 1719 novel. Or visualize Mowgli, the protagonist of Rudyard Kipling's Victorian novel *The Jungle Book,* published in 1894. That child becomes an adolescent without having any contact with anyone from London, New Delhi, or anywhere in the so-called civilized world. What kinds of dreams might he have? Because you would agree with me that, even without existing in a society where there is a strong superego—the category Freud employed to refer to the moral code the individual needs to adjust to—he still dreams every night. And while there might not be anyone nearby to describe those dreams, he in fact has a healthy dream existence.

IJ: So?

IS: For the purposes of our discussion, let's set the time of our hypothetical tale in 2001. Does he dream with automobiles? No. Movies, iPods, text messages, and the Internet? No. A magazine? No. Perhaps something simpler: a fork, a knife, and a spoon? He is able to dream only with objects he's aware of because the limits of our language—and here I'm talking about the grammar of dreams—are the limits of our world. Stretching it, our protagonist might be able to visualize a twelve-legged crocodile with the face of a lion and the wings of a parrot. In his universe, such creature isn't usual so he'll be fearful of it. He'll believe it is a monster!

IJ: I understand your point. But how does it go from the island to a civilization?

IS: Each civilization has its own idiosyncrasy. That idiosyncrasy manifests itself in the dreams its people have on a regular basis. The challenge, Iván, is that, as you and I have been arguing, some of us are immigrants. And the dreams immigrants have are hybrids . . .

IJ: Because we transpose ourselves from one civilization to another.

IS: Yes. I'm convinced that in the journey an immigrant undertakes, the metamorphosis of her dreams is directly proportional to the change in her surroundings.

IJ: I'm not sure. As an immigrant from Chile to the United States, I had dreams early on that included a plane. I didn't care if it was an aircraft made in my home country or in the United States.

IS: Probably you wouldn't have dreamed about an airplane had you not arrived in one. And you certainly would not dream about one if airplanes had not been invented yet. Anyway, I too have reservations about these thoughts.

IJ: What kinds of dreams did you have upon arriving to New York? If I remember properly, in *On Borrowed Words* you mention one in which you and your father were in a jungle.

IS: Yes, and a threatening indigenous tribe captured us. I remember also having dreams in which I was jumping from one tree to another in a tundra. It wasn't a forest per se. It looked to me like a scene from a film by Andrei Tarkovsky I saw once that took place in Siberia.

IJ: Do you see those dreams as Hispanic?

IS: I'm not sure. How about you?

IJ: We're all both part of a unique civilization or culture, and universal human beings with similar reactions to day-to-day events or long-term fears and desires. So my inclination would be to say no, there is no difference, and to say along with Longfellow about dreams that "they lift us from the commonplace of life to better things" regardless of where we come from. I suppose he was not thinking about nightmares, but I would agree with him that dreams, in a narrow sense, are probably very pleasant projections or resolutions that reconcile us with the disappointments of life. But most of my own dreams are not pleasant: they involve dilemmas, confusions, and befuddlements. One dream has always been constant, and consistently pleasant: running, running to the point that I no longer feel my body. The flip side of the dream-coin is that of not being able to run, as in a swamp, or stuck in something while needing to escape. But to honor your question, can we have dreams that are peculiar to a culture or civilization? Yes, to the extent that we dream in a language. I know, you have already told me that that is not your case, that your experience is one of situations and understandings beyond words. But words have been important in my case, and sometimes my dreams revolve around certain words, either in English or in Spanish. Sometimes I have been able to reconstruct the dream and figure out that in a daytime situation I was grasping for a word, which somehow reappeared in a dream.

As a historian, I usually go through tons of private letters or diaries by historical figures. But dreams are rarely mentioned. When you encounter them, however, they are so valuable. I remember I understood Andrés Bello's nostalgia for his homeland when he referred to a dream he had in 1856 about Caracas and "some very dear people at that happy time in our youth." He was referring to feelings and memories from nearly half a century before. I also recall a dream mentioned by the Colombian Rafael Pombo, who adored Longfellow and dreamed that he had seen him in his Cambridge home. He told the poet, "I dreamed I was in your house, talking in Spanish to your daughters, and when you came in, you told me, 'You look very much like a jeweler.'" Pombo interpreted this quite positively, although I find the comment most puzzling.

IS: Iván, I had a dream last night. I dreamed that you were a James Bond type, jet-setting from one casino to another, and I was following you, although clumsily.

IJ: What do you mean?

IS: You would arrive at the next casino in stylish fashion, whereas

I would almost fall down from a boat on which we were sailing, or slip from a rock in an alpine mountain. Upon making it to the next destination, you always looked elegant. In contrast, I was a wreck . . .

IJ: I doubt that Hollywood will cast me as the next James Bond, but thanks for the idea! But really, Ilan, isn't the dream a confirmation of a space beyond culture that in some fashion speaks to our itinerant collaboration and lives? If I start counting the places where we have been writing this book, we would have to mention at least three continents and several countries. And we have missed each other on a couple of occasions by just a few days or even hours, as when you were in Amherst and I briefly in Boston. Or when you left New York City the day before I arrived. Or when my cell phone failed while I was calling you from Buffalo. This is the sort of predicament that would have been unthinkable just a few decades ago. But today we move with a speed that challenges any sort of sense of roots and belonging. To go back to our epigraph by Ryszard Kapuściński, aren't we fast particles, moving in some orbit but intersecting with others, all the while aware that we are not alone, and have never been, in this universe? Our hispanidad is rooted in a changing tradition, flexible enough to persist beyond boundaries and circumstances. Let us not fix it with a definition but allow it instead to travel, always.

ILAN STAVANS is the Lewis-Sebring Professor in Latin American and Latino Culture and Five College 40th Anniversary Professor at Amherst College. His books include *The Hispanic Condition* (1995), *The Riddle of Cantinflas* (1998), *On Borrowed Words* (2001), *Spanglish* (2003), *Dictionary Days* (2005), *The Disappearance* (2006), *Love and Language* (2007), *Resurrecting Hebrew* (2008), *A Critic's Journey* (2009), and *Gabriel García Márquez: The Early Years* (2010). He edited *The Oxford Book of Jewish Stories* (1998), *The Poetry of Pablo Neruda* (2004), *Isaac Bashevis Singer: Collected Stories* (3 vols., 2004), *Encyclopedia Latina* (4 vols., 2005), *The Schocken Book of Modern Sephardic Literature* (2005), *César Vallejo: "Spain, Take This Chalice from Me" and Other Poems* (2008), *Cesar Chavez: An Organizer's Tale* (2008), *Becoming Americans: Four Centuries of Immigrant Writing* (2009), *The Norton Anthology of Latino Literature* (2010), and *The FSG Book of 20th-Century Latin American Poetry* (2011). His story "Morirse está en hebreo" was made into the award-winning movie *My Mexican Shivah* (2007), produced by John Sayles. Stavans has received numerous awards, among them a Guggenheim Fellowship, the National Jewish Book Award, the Latino Book Award, Chile's Presidential Medal, and the Rubén Darío Distinction. His work has been translated into a dozen languages.

IVÁN JAKSIĆ is a professor of history at the Catholic University of Chile and the director of the Stanford University Bing Overseas Studies Program in Santiago. He is the author of *Academic Rebels in Chile: The Role of Philosophy in Higher Education and Politics* (1989), *Andrés Bello: Scholarship and Nation-Building in Nineteenth-Century Latin America* (2001), and *The Hispanic World and American Intellectual Life, 1820–1880* (2007). He is editor or coeditor of *Filosofía e iden-*

tidad cultural en América Latina (1988), *The Struggle for Democracy in Chile* (1991, revised 1995), *Sarmiento: Author of a Nation* (1994), *Selected Writings of Andrés Bello* (1997), *El modelo chileno* (1999), and *The Political Power of the Word: Press and Oratory in Nineteenth-Century Latin America* (2002). His book on Bello has been published in Spanish in Venezuela and Chile (three editions, 2001–2010) and received the prize "Pensamiento de América" from the Pan American Institute of Geography and History in Mexico. An elected fellow of the Massachusetts Historical Society, he is also recipient of fellowships from the Guggenheim Foundation, the National Endowment for the Humanities, and the Ford Foundation and has been a visiting scholar at Harvard and a senior associate member at Oxford University.

INDEX